CONTEMPORARY
ROME
VIEWED THROUGH HISTORY

CONTEMPORARY
ROME
VIEWED THROUGH HISTORY

DR CLIVE GILLIS

AMBASSADOR

BELFAST, NORTHERN IRELAND
GREENVILLE, SOUTH CAROLINA

Contemporary Rome Viewed Through History
© 2003 Dr Clive Gillis

ISBN 1 84030 140 6

PRINTED IN NORTHERN IRELAND

Published by
Ambassador Productions Ltd.,
Providence House
Ardenlee Street,
Belfast, BT6 8QJ
www.ambassador-productions.com

Emerald House Group Inc.
427 Wade Hampton Boulevard,
Greenville,
South Carolina 29609
www.emeraldhouse.com

Contents

About the Author

Dr. Clive Gillis is married with two grown up sons. He works as a full time General Medical Practitioner near Bristol. He was born again in 1963 while attending Medical School in Leeds. He attends the Free Presbyterian Church in Bristol, England.

Dr. Gillis' interest in Church history was stimulated by the writings of the Reformers and Puritans on the historicist view of the Book of Revelation, and by widespread travel on the Continent.

Dr. Gillis not only visited the martyr sites as many others have done, but also attempted to trace the places in Rome where remains recording these events - often in the most haughty fashion - may still be seen, albeit with increasing difficulty.

In the course of these trips, Dr. Gillis was struck with the lack of contemporary Protestant literature. So when the opportunity arose to submit articles to the *English Churchman*, Dr. Gillis was able to make a contribution in this respect. The articles are journalistic rather than academic. Readers have commented that they would like this information in a more convenient and permanent form for easier reference, and one which would reach a wider audience hence the publication of this book.

Acknowledgements

I should like to thank Dr Paisley and the Free Presbyterian Church of Ulster for their interest in publishing the work of an unknown author. I am indebted to Dr. Napier Malcolm of the English Churchman for his unstinting patience and meticulous editing to produce a clear presentation of the material with the conversion of any dreary prose into crisp journalism, without ever attempting to modify the text.

I am grateful under God to the Evangelist Edgar Parkyns, now with the Lord, who introduced me to the historicist interpretation of the Book of Revelation. I must thank the Protestant Alliance for showing me how much can be learnt by travel. I am indebted to the librarians of the Bridgwater Library who have turned up treasurers time and time again. They have also negotiated with the lenders to relieve me of the necessity of reading them on the premises, which was out of the question because of the nature of my work. I am particularly grateful to Shelia Atkinson for allowing these valuable texts to be collected from the Mobile Library. I must also thank my wife who has suffered my writing, proof read and criticised, been robbed and mugged with the author in Rome and many a time insisted we press on up some tortuous and precipitous part of Church history trail to gain the prize, when the more timid author was for turning back.

Foreword
by Dr. Ian R K Paisley MP MEP MLA

The Papacy cannot be understood nor its real nature assessed without careful study of its history.

History is the great condemning witness against the Papacy. Ignorance of her history will keep us in a state of deception. A knowledge of her history will so expose Vaticanism that we will turn away from the Papacy amazed at her devilish deception of the nations of the earth.

The prophecies of Holy Scripture have warned us of a religious system claiming to be true Christianity, but is in reality Antichrist which will deceive the nations of the whole earth.

In the plainest language the Word of God uncovers the apostasy, corruption and abominations of the Popes and their politico-religion. What more succinct statements could we find anywhere else than in the prophetic Scriptures.

The abysmal ignorance of our generation as to the real nature of Rome is simply staggering. The success of the Vatican propaganda machine has been startling.

The constant white-washing of their words, deeds and atrocities by the Church of Rome is amazing. How telling is the description of the Bible, *'the mystery of iniquity.'* - What a penetrating summary!

Dr. Clive Gillis, the author of this important and well-researched book, has shone the light of history upon the Papacy.

Along with irrefutable facts he has marshalled an invincible army of unchallengeable arguments for the Scriptural and historical view of the Papacy.

He invites us to behold the Papacy in the penetrating light of history so that we can be aware of what the Papacy really is - not the only true Church of Christ upon earth, as she claims to be, but rather the greatest of all religious counterfeits which the Holy Scripture foretold would come.

It was the Grand Old Man, William Gladstone, Prime Minister of England, who said of Roman Catholic education, *'No more cunning plot was ever devised, at least by man, against the freedom, the happiness and the virtue of mankind.'*

This invaluable book is the antidote for that well executed cunning plot of the Papacy.

Archbishop Whately on the same subject of Roman Catholic education said, *'Nothing could exceed the unblushing audacity of its falsehoods, except the atrocity of its principles and the perversions of its morals is still worse than its perversion of the facts.'*

How powerfully this has been exposed in the paedophile priests of Rome and those who would shield them today.

This book can enable its readers to know the truth and the truth can make them FREE.

Dr. Graham Scroggie, the renowned Bible teacher, once said, *'Rome wants a reunited Christendom, but only by the capitulation of all the Churches to herself. The fox has no objection to the geese, provided they are all **inside** her. But a reunited Christendom on these terms would be the greatest blunder and crime in the history of religion.'*

It is because of that great curse to which the Papacy is heading that this publication is a must for every Protestant home.

Ian R. K. Paisley
Eph 6: 19+20

House of Commons, Westminster
March 2003

CHAPTER ONE

Rome's Savaging Saints and Maiming Madonnas

The first time the present writer set out for Prague to walk in the footsteps of John Huss, he had little conception of how much Counter Reformation Romanism still survives there.

Hence a visit to St. James (Kostel Svateho Jakoba) turned out to be rather a surprise. This is a baroque Counter-Reformation church, just off Old Town Square. The Huss interest lies in the fact that, in 1412, three young men Martin, John and Stasek (pro-

St. James Church, Prague where three Protestants were arrested.

nounced 'stashe') were peacefully protesting outside about the sale of indulgences, when they were arrested and put in prison in the Old

Town Hall. The next day, July 12th, Huss tried to intervene for clemency which appeared to be granted, but as soon as he left, all three were beheaded.

The people, who were then largely sympathetic to the reform movement, were furious, and carried the men's bodies to Bethlehem chapel with shouts of "these men are martyrs". Huss conducted a Martyr's Mass in defiance of the Vatican, whose sole prerogative it was to hold such a service, and buried them decently in the chapel. This was one of the accusations later levelled against Huss at his trial in Constance. There is nothing to see now, but the spirit of Protestantism stirs within one, when reflecting upon these things on the very spot where they actually occurred.

A gruesome reminder

On leaving the church, this reverie was suddenly disturbed by the sight of a cadaverous human forearm to the left of the entrance, dangling from the ceiling on a long chain.

It seems that in about 1400 AD a thief went to steal the jewels on the high altar which had been presented as a votive offering to the Madonna. The outraged Virgin seized the thief's forearm and would not let go, despite the intercessions of the priests. The only thing to do was to amputate the arm, which is depicted in a nearby painting. The arm was subsequently hung up on the chain as a warning to others.

It is easy to be impressed by the cunning security system of the priests and pass on and forget the matter. However, it is worth stopping for a moment to consider the mindset of the devotees of popular Romanism. How does it come about that "Our Lady", represented as so gentle and loving, is nevertheless, capable of tearing the arm off a living man?

The recent deaths of hundreds of members of the 'Restoration of the Ten Commandments of God' cult in their church building at Kanungu in Uganda has made this aspect of Romanism topical. Six of the leading members of the group were nuns and priests that had been excommunicated. Many others were former Roman Catholics who were simply perpetuating in the new cult the beliefs of popular Roman Catholicism in the area. Numerous icons of madonnas and Roman

The severed arm.

Catholic saints were found in the compound. People in the surrounding villages said that after two date setting failures for Christ's return, the sect (which all news reports stressed was strongly Roman Catholic in character) expected the Virgin Mary to appear. According to some reports she did appear to "carry them to heaven". In any event the Virgin presided over their immolation.

Italian Cult of Mary

The Cult of the Virgin Mary has been extensively studied by Michael P. Carroll who is Professor of Sociology at the University of Western Ontario. His aim is to explain the harmful effects of madonnas and "saints" in terms of Freudian psychology. As a social scientist he ignores the reality of Satan and evil spirits. But his extensive research and concern for detail demand attention. Rome takes exception to his work, dismissing it as "preposterous and simplistic", despite it being published by the prestigious Princeton and John Hopkins University press. His hard hitting study *Madonnas that Maim* has had a wide circulation and it has particularly irritated Rome. Michael Carroll is descended from Italian, Roman Catholic,

The maiming Madonna in St. James Church, Prague.

immigrants who came to America in the middle of the last century. He has taken a great interest in his roots and studied in Italy and is therefore thoroughly conversant with the Italian language.

Carroll's studies have provoked controversy because he has broken new ground - at least for Anglo-Saxons - in the field of Italian church history, even though this is not his speciality.

To date, most of the information available in English about the history of popular Roman Catholicism in Southern Italy, has come from one of three sources. There are the studies by English anthropologists of certain Italian communities. These tend to be local and lack historical perspective. There are studies of Italian immigrant communities in America but, inevitably, tradition becomes corrupted and historical recall is unreliable. English church histories do exist but they are usually either academic and specialised or they are 18th and 19th century Protestant propaganda and open to accusation of bias.

Carroll stumbled upon a wealth of history, some not translated into English. He comments: "I can do little about the general failure to translate the most important Italian language works", but he hopes, he "will pique the interest of sufficient readers to create a demand for their translation".

Spiritual hierarchy

The Papacy and the curia are predominantly Italian. From 1417-1978, 56 of the 59 popes were Italians and the folk religion of this little Mediterranean peninsula now affects the lives of many millions of people throughout the world. Yet, even in the 21st century the story of its roots is not easily available in English.

When Carroll speaks of "popular historical Roman Catholicism", he means all religious practices involving the magical or supernatural that are tolerated by the official Roman Catholic hierarchy. Emilio Sereni in his *History of the Italian Agricultural Landscape* is particularly concerned with the Middle Ages. He writes, "Among God, the Madonna and the saints, the peasant in Sicily and many parts of the Mezzogiorno (Southern Italy) has, in his own way, established a kind of hierarchy: Christ is more powerful than God the Father, Mary is more powerful than Christ ... But more powerful than God ... all the saints ... is the inhabitant's Patron Saint, the God of the place to whom the peasant turns in times of despair".

They are created, not by legend, but by the action of the Roman hierarchy, who provide the original stimulus for the cult. Thus , to take one instance, the town fathers of Loreto Aprunito on the Adriatic coast opposite Rome, have all their tourist attractions posted in English on the internet. A priority for the visitor is the church of San Pietro Apostolo which boasts a silver urn containing San Zopito's relics. Their website announces on Whitsunday and Monday: "The Feast of Zopito, during which a white ox, ridden by a child in white robes, is obliged to kneel down before the Saint's statue and then follows it into the church". San Zopito is absent from most church dictionaries because he is only one of many local saints little known in the English speaking world. The cult has gripped the town and surrounding area for 300 years but has now been toned down.

The full ceremony consisted of the ox genuflecting on the church threshold on Whitsunday. It was then taken to all the residents. The following day the ox, carrying the boy in white, had to genuflect before San Zopito's reliquary right inside the church. Mass was then celebrated. A grand procession followed with the ox, a silver statue of San Zopito, musicians and banners. The ox had to genuflect at each of the town's churches. The peasants believed that the success of the following year's harvest depended on whether and how much the ox defecated. Defecation inside the church was a particularly propitious sign for a peasantry to whom the harvest was everything. A priest who tried to modify the ceremonial in 1876 caused a riot which it required infantry to quell. He collapsed during the disturbance and his death was seen as the saint's retribution.

Sospitus in Domino

Pope Clement XI had initiated the cult by sending a martyr's bone from the catacomb of San Callisto in Rome in 1710 at the request of the local priests. They felt that a progressive town should have a relic. A funeral tablet bore the word 'zospitus'. This was probably just the standard Latin inscription 'Sospitus in Domino' ('Sleep in the Lord'), which they mistook for a proper name. The relics arrived on the Monday after Pentecost which became the saint's day. The priests promoted the saint, "miracles" multiplied and the patronal powers of St. Zopito grew in popular superstitious esteem. Deliverance from demons was linked with the ox ritual and developed into an elaborate local folk religion beyond the control of the clergy. This resulted in vengeance when a priest tried to curb it.

Carroll has uncovered many similar examples in the Italian literature, and as each locality has a saint, the total number in rural Italy must be very high.

The Virgin Mary is already a legitimate object of devotion, so no further approbation by the priests is required. But by a process similar to the one just described, specific local Madonnas also tend to evolve. They have little in common with Rome's official Mary. These local madonnas gain the same awesome hold over the community as the patron saints. The madonnas are seen as a sisterhood, and are numerous in southern Italy. An old peasant woman once wisely advised an aspiring priest to "know his madonnas", as they all have distinct but specific magical powers. These are often indicated by their titles, (*delle grazie* - favours; *deli miracoli* - miracles; *del soccorso* - help). They also attract numerous pilgrims, who know their powers better than the priests, and who search them out to meet needs not catered for by their own local saints and madonnas. All this indigenous activity is beyond the control of the priests, who simply manipulate it to their own advantage.

'The dark side of holiness'

Rome's displeasure with Carroll stems from his making available to English readers the frightening, dual, benevolent/malevolent influence of these madonnas and saints. He calls it "the dark side of holiness". Implicit in the Madonna's first apparition is always the veiled threat "build a church in my honour ... or else". Woe betide the local priest who does not rally to the visionary's report of the Madonna's demand! Priests who have refused and who were subsequently maimed or died a sudden death have provided a powerful incentive to others not to follow their example. This dire retribution is also meted out to worshippers who insult the cult madonna. In 1589 two peasants, Aurelia and Marco del Prete, were queuing with an ex-votive at the shrine of the Madonna dell Arco during her festa to thank her for curing Marco's eye disease, when Aurelia's prized piglet escaped, and with it a much needed source of future family sustenance. Indignant, Aurelia mouthed blasphemies at the madonna and trampled the ex-votive under foot. One year later, on the night before the next festa, Aurelia's feet detached from her legs. The mindset of the cult is preserved in an inscription on the cornerstone of the sanctuary "To the Madonna dell'Arco (in reparation) for the blasphemer Aurelia who was punished in her feet (*castigati nei piedi*) on the 20th day of April in the year 1590". A young man who, in pique threw a ball at her, making her cheek bleed, paid with his life for his insulting behaviour.

For anyone wishing to visit this capricious goddess, she too has her details on the internet.

Sometimes a maiming madonna can be appeased. A soldier urinated over an image of the Madonna del Popolo in Bologna and in retribution was blinded and afflicted with excruciating pain "in the parts that offended the Madonna". He repented and was miraculously healed. The saint San Donato of Montesano in Italy's heel is also on the internet. He specialises in the cure of epilepsy. But prospective pilgrims should take care. When Anabella Rossi interviewed devotees

The Iron Virgin of Nuremberg

at the 1956 festa, she learned that "the sickness of San Donato - 'he sends it, the saint sends it'. The afflicted scream night and day ... 'the blessed San Donato sends all nervous diseases, all of them ... Every saint sends his illness and (so) holds on to his devotion'".

The revisionist Cambridge church historian Eamon Duffy, ever ready with a defence when he sees Rome under attack, responded to Carroll in his 1999 Aquinas Lecture to the Dominican's of Blackfriars, Glasgow. He found his task difficult. At one point he comments, "By now you may be thinking I have come here to present the case for the prosecution against the Blessed Virgin ... the character of much of the Marian piety of the last two centuries does indeed appear uncomfortably vulnerable to the accusations levelled against it by its critics". He gave few cogent arguments against Carroll.

We only differ from Carroll in that he seeks an explanation from Freud, where we see Satan and his devilish host at work.

Carroll's work provides a strong argument against the revisionists such as Professor Kamen of Barcelona who see the Iron Maiden of the Inquisition as mere Protestant propaganda. These life-sized, hinged, metal madonnas with internal spikes which are said to have tortured heretics while the Madonna embraced them, have come down in numbers in public and private collections and the author has seen several on his travels. They stand in need of *some* explanation.

Belief in this monstrous ambivalence of the Virgin, this curious mixture of benevolence and malevolence in her ministrations, is deeply embedded in the Roman Catholic psyche. The Inquisitors would see nothing inconsistent in using this form of torture in the name of Mary. This was how they understood her and indeed how they understood the world over which she presided.

CHAPTER TWO

Hidden Fears and Secret Occult Rites: The Vatican - A Windswept City?

The Church of Rome would seem to be triumphant on the eve of the new millennium. As she entered 1999 the popular Catholic press carried headlines like: "Catholic numbers break all previous records", proclaiming that the world's Roman Catholic population had now passed the one billion mark.

The Vatican had the pleasure of announcing this when it unveiled the 1999 Vatican year book in a special presentation to Pope John Paul II in February.

The church's pastoral work force totals 3.4 million. There are more than 404,000 priests world wide. Despite his age, the present Pope can attract crowds in excess of one million when he visits a Catholic country anywhere in the world. As a state amongst states, the Vatican now maintains diplomatic relations with 168 countries. This too is a record.

Likewise, when the wraps come off at the end of the year, Rome's basilicas and numerous lesser Churches are set to shine with a brilliance not seen for generations. This is in readiness to greet the anticipated influx of millions of millennial pilgrims seeking the benefits both of the relics which will be on display and of the Jubilee indulgence which has already been announced.

Indeed, Rome may well say, "I sit as a queen, and am no widow, and shall see no sorrow".

Priestly lifestyles

However, all is not quite as happy as it seems. Like many another house built upon sand, when the wind blows and beats upon it, Rome must fall. To take one instance, Rome's alarm at the declining number of vocations to the priesthood is well known. Ireland, with one of the lowest ratios of Catholics per priest in the world at 774 (Brazil 8729 for every priest) was reported by *The Universe* in October 1998 to have sustained a 50% fall in priest, nun and brother numbers over the past 10 years. Disappointing figures for Mass attendance, which the Pope in his Apostolic letter *Dies Domini* ('The Day of the Lord') described as central to the Catholic commitment, were glossed over earlier this year as "somewhat mixed". In fact, independent surveys have shown that the attendance at Mass is considerably lower in many countries than the figures claimed by Rome. Thus in Poland, the Pope's home country, where mass attendance is regarded as almost one hundred per cent, a recent independent survey showed it to have fallen by 33 per cent. The *Guardian* reported on the 7th May that one month before the Pope's forthcoming visit, Polish priests had been warned to give up their "luxury lifestyles". A report from Poland's national synod states that, "The clergy's luxury lifestyles are a cause of shame as are their smart cars, their high fees for pastoral services and their lack of understanding of many families financial problems". In the same month an independent survey showed that one quarter (26%) of Poles did not trust the Roman Catholic Church and that two thirds said they believed the Church was too political.

"Secret sins and vices"

This growing, widespread, scepticism amongst Catholics is fuelled by the continuing scandals at home and abroad. In the same week as I write, the *Times* reported a new Spanish initiative to rewrite the history of the legendary immorality and financial greed of Borgia Pope Alexander VI. And yet, the same newspaper had to run the headline:

"Vatican in fight to ban sex expose" as stories surface of priestly immorality on a par with the Borgia scandals. Richard Owen, the *Times* Rome correspondent, reveals that the Vatican is taking legal action in an attempt to suppress a "scandalous" book by a Vatican insider which discloses the alleged "secret sins and vices" of Cardinals and other senior Roman Catholic churchmen of a kind entirely reminiscent of the time of the Borgias. This 300 page book *Via Col Vento in Vaticano* or 'Gone with the wind in the Vatican', appears under a pseudonym. Rome is accusing a recently retired senior churchman, Monsignor Luigi Marinelli, from the Congregation of Oriental Churches of being the author, and he now faces the threat of excommunication. Owen reports that this was portrayed in the Italian newspaper *Corriere della Sera* as a reflection of a deadly power struggle within the Curia in the twilight years of the present Pope.

Dark clouds over the Vatican.

Malachi Martin

As headline after headline in the popular Catholic press brings news of new sexual immorality, of child abuse, of venerable seminaries without applications for the priesthood, of financial scandals and of modern innovations on every side, one senses the perplexity of traditional Roman Catholics. No doubt, many older folk look back fondly to the days before the Second Vatican Council and ponder whether Rome's evils stem from that time. Sensing, no doubt, the commercial potential of this unease, an Irish Roman Catholic bookseller placed a large advertisement in the popular English Catholic press at the beginning of the year. It was headed, "A timely and urgently needed viewpoint on the state of the Church and the Papacy". It advertised a book *Windswept House* by the popular writer Malachi Martin, an ex-Jesuit. The advert poses the question, "When faced with falling vocations and Church attendances, our hopes remain buoyant with our vision of the future Church. Catholics appear to be so inured to these trends that when such scandals as homosexuality and paedophilia among the clergy raise their ugly heads, the most relevant question remains unasked. That questions is Why? Perhaps, belatedly, *Windswept House*, makes the link between the experience of time and those questions, and to surprisingly good effect".

Not wishing to obtain a copy from a Roman Catholic source, I instigated an internet search and to my amazement the book came up on a list of booksellers specialising in magic, the occult and witchcraft.

Windswept House

To understand the background of *Windswept House*, it is necessary to know that there has been a period of great dissension behind the walls of the Vatican during the present Pope's pontificate. Peter Stanford, the Catholic journalist, recently interviewed on television, said that, "this Pope will go down in history as a great pope for the world, but that he will go down as a bad pope for the Catholic Church ... itself ... because he has caused divisions and dissensions". This is why articles have begun to appear in the Catholic press stressing papal supreme authority and why Catholic traditionalists are expressing concern about the idea that authority should be exercised in the future by the Church itself at the expense of the Pope's primacy.

Malachi Martin writes *Windswept House* as a novel, but he has an immense knowledge of the inner workings of the Vatican as one would expect of an ex-Secretary to Cardinal Bea, who was the architect of the ecumenical movement at the Second Vatican Council. Martin was also a Professor at Rome's Pontifical Bible Institute. He is to the inner world of the Vatican what John Le Carre is to the world of espionage. Martin's thinly disguised characters and situations display his insider knowledge. He teases his audience by feeding in sensitive information here and there, then leaving them to guess how much is fact rather than fiction, knowing that, in the light of so many past statements that have been proved to be fact, readers will be slow to dismiss what he says as fiction. His present novel is no exception. The powers of evil are represented by a deep desire to overthrow the "good" papal primacy and replace it by an evil one world system, of which the Church, divorced of papal primacy, is an important element.

Enthronement of Lucifer

But what makes this novel of such interest to devotees of the occult is, that Martin prefaces it with a 27 page historical prologue resting his whole reputation on the fact that what he states there, however outrageous it may sound, is potentially verifiable and must be true. According to Martin, on 29th June 1963, "The enthronement of the Fallen Archangel Lucifer was effected" within the Vatican itself, only days after the enthronement of Paul VI. This was in response to a strongly held Satanist tradition which predicted that the "Time of the Prince" would be ushered in at the moment when a pope would take the name of the Apostle Paul, there having been no Paul since 1621. A ritual black mass is described in horrific detail though somewhat confusing as two ceremonies are taking place at once. The Vatican is the recipient chapel while another in America is the targeting chapel, where the agonising violation of a small girl Agness by one of the priests occurs. The leading priest is clearly following a detailed liturgy invoking Satan with such responses as, "I believe in the Only Begotten Son of the Cosmic Dawn," and, "Come, take possession of the enemy's house. Enter into a place that has been prepared for you." Martin records among the closing words spoken at the Roman end of the ritual, "By mandate of the Assembly of the sacrosanct elders, I do institute, authorise and recognise this Chapel, to be known henceforth as the Inner Chapel, as taken, possessed and appropriated wholly by

Him Whom we have Enthroned as Lord and Master of our human fate". This event is seen by some as the explanation of a strange comment by Paul VI in the mid seventies that, "the smoke of Satan has entered the Vatican".

New rite of exorcism

Martin goes on to present evidence that before the death of John XXIII, the predecessor of Paul VI, died, he had gathered information upon Satanism within the Vatican and passed it on to his successors. Many Protestants have laboured to demonstrate the occult basis of the Church of Rome, showing how the practices of ancient Babylon and Egypt were absorbed over a period of time. As the early Church began to fall away, they slowly found their way into Romish ceremonial and architecture. Sadly, in today's ecumenical climate such writings are often considered irrelevant, if not actually offensive. However, the fact that no official response to Martin's book has been made, suggests that his information is probably accurate.

One wonders whether the new rite of exorcism, which has been updated in the light of the Second Vatican Council (the previous one having been introduced in 1614), is an attempt to discredit the suggestion that Satanism is a reality in the Vatican and has a hold on it. The New Rite, of which the Latin version is entitled *De exorcism et supplicationibus quibusdam*, was presented by Cardinal Jorge Arturo Medina Estevez, Prefect of the Congregation of Divine Worship, at a press conference on 26th January 1999.

However, on the following day, the Cardinal presented a *Notification* bearing his signature stating that the congregation "by virtue of a special faculty granted it by the Supreme Pontiff," will, "willingly" grant bishops who request it, a faculty "for the priest entrusted with the task of exorcism, to use the rite under Title XII of the Roman Rite closed 1952 edition", thus making the traditional rite still valid.

Perhaps there is a fear in some quarters that the modern rite may not be equal to the task if the Vatican were to find itself in real conflict with Satanists!

The Vatican is a windswept city indeed.

CHAPTER THREE

The Padre Pio Phenomenon - Modern Miracle or Medieval Superstition?

The 19ᵗʰ of May 1980 was a turning point in the life of South Yorkshire housewife Alice Jones.

Father Fisher of St. Matthew's Anglican Church, Sheffield, had arranged to visit Alice despite her protestations that she "did not want anything to do with the church or Christ any more". Her bitterness stemmed from an accident many years previously which had "crushed the spinal nerves". Her husband, Frank, a retired orthopaedic nurse, had stood with her through numerous operations and treatments only to see her pain worsen and her left leg wither. This homely Northern couple's story, entitled *Working Miracles*, was widely shown on National TV in the early 90s and subsequently released as a home video.

First time in seven years

In the video Alice describes Father Fisher's visits to her home with an intensity that is spellbinding. The first time he prayed Alice felt her spine "warm". There followed a night of intercession. The next day, as Father Fisher ministered, Alice saw "just in front of him ... another face ... an older man with a beard ... and very brown eyes ... in a long robe and a girdle". She thought, "It must be Father Gabriel the other parish priest". Then "He took over ... blessed me twice ... in a foreign language ... and said, 'Arise in the name of Jesus, get up and walk'. I got out of that chair for the first time in seven years and walked".

Authentic Francis of Assisi with stigmata. [Close up in circle]

Later on, Father Fisher passed her a prayer card bearing the image of a dead Italian Capuchin Friar, Francesco Forgione, now known as Padre Pio. He was a stigmatic - that is, he bore the wounds of Christ in his body. She realised at once that this was the man who had appeared with Father Fisher and healed her. Even when she discovered, that he had died in 1968, she still insisted, "This man was real ... I could feel the knot in his girdle". Father Fisher was further able to authenticate the miracle because, "when Padre Pio is around there is a perfume present ... The first thing I remember was the very strong aftershave ... I don't have any aftershave".

Perfume and bilocation

The significance of this is made clear by Father McQueeny, Spiritual Director of the Padre Pio Foundation of America, who explains that besides the "stigmata" whereby, "Padre Pio bore the wounds of Christ for 50 years", he also had the gifts of perfume, miraculous cures and bilocation (the ability to be in two places at once).

Alice Jones down-to-earth Englishness must have done much to overcome the innate wariness of Southern European Catholicism that exists even among Roman Catholics. It also helped to promote interest in Padre Pio in Protestant circles, particularly when she gave her testimony in Liverpool Cathedral.

Padre Pio's following is now immense. The *Universe* reported on the 4th October 1988 that "More pilgrims visit his tomb than go either to Lourdes or Fatima ... In 1997 alone, 7.5 million people prayed at his tomb while 6 million visited Lourdes and only 2 million Fatima". The Vatican pronounced him 'Venerable' on the 18th December 1997 and he is due to be beatified in great splendour at St. Peter's Rome on the 2nd May 1999. Besides a myriad of books, articles and videos there is now a Padre Pio website, replete with information and, incidentally, a warning of "misinformation about Padre Pio". However, there are two public documents which Rome must stand by. They are the Catholic Truth Society booklet and the text of the Veneration Decree.

Subsisted on wafer

Born of simple farming stock in Pietrelcina in Southern Italy in 1887, Pio was always inclined to mysticism. He was ordained in 1910 into the severe Capuchin order and went from "friary to friary". His ecstasies, his self-starvation through subsistence on the wafer alone and his self-flagellation, "left him perched on the edge of death". He came eventually to San Giovanni Rotundo at the heel of Italy, between

Foggia and the Adriatic Sea, where he remained until his death. It was here, kneeling before a crucifix in the Friary of our Lady of Grace on the 20th September 1918, that he received the "Stigmata", the wounds of Christ's Crucifixion, in his palms, feet and side.

Priceless relic

These painful wounds bled a cup of blood each day and his hands were always covered with mittens except at mass and in an official Vatican photograph of 1919. His mittens, dressings and even the crusts of dried blood which fell from his hands are all preserved at San Giovanni, close to his tomb for veneration. Indeed, Father Alessio Parenti brought a mitten in a suitable polythene cover to anoint the faithful on the occasion of Alice Jones' testimony in Liverpool Cathedral.

Further, Stella Lilly of the English Padre Pio Centre showed one of the crusts on national Television which she wears in a reliquary round her neck. She explained that after Padre Pio's beatification it will become a priceless first-class relic. As vast crowds are expected in San Giovanni for the Millennium, Rome has engaged the world famous architect Renzo Piano to design a vast new church to which Pio's body and relics will be transferred to mark the year 2000.

A close reading of the Veneration Decree alongside the older Catholic Truth Society pamphlet shows a toning down of certain aspects of his life. The Catholic Truth Society talks of "things that made prudent, godly men uneasy". The Veneration Decree speaks only of "virtues". The Catholic Truth Society refers to, "ecstasies - long held suspect as possible delusions or self-indulgences", the Veneration Decree only of "absorption in supernatural realities". The Catholic Truth Society states that he was "of little practical use to any community which he joined", the Veneration Decree only that he "rested among his brothers". In particular the Veneration Decree fails to refer to the question of his having evaded conscription in the First World War, when he went absent without leave, while the Catholic Truth Society states that "the police were actually sent to pick him up and return him as a deserter", a mistake attributed to "military confusion over his file".

Wealth to region

The Archbishop of nearby Manfredonia started his enquiries into the life of Padre Pio in 1973. The official Vatican enquiry inaugurating the path to Canonisation began in 1983, and "could take centuries or 20 years," according to the Catholic Truth Society. The success of Padre Pio's case to date must be due at least in part, to his popularity and also the wealth he has brought to a poor region. San Giovanni's opulent marbled hospital, the Casa Sollievo Della Sofferenzia, has become, by reputation, one of the finest in Italy. And the new church will further multiply the benefits available to pilgrims willing to spend their money.

Paul in his Epistle to the Galatians (6:17) said "I bear in my body the marks (Greek: 'stigmata') of the Lord Jesus". Luther considered these to be, "His sufferings and stripes" from the stonings and beatings which he endured for the Gospel's sake. Likewise, Calvin asks, "What were those marks?" He answers, "Every injurious treatment he had incurred in bearing testimony to the Gospel".

The first major instance of "stigmata" to mimic Christ's wounds occurred in Francis of Assisi on the Feast of the Exaltation of The Holy Cross in 1224. By 1909 Dr. Imbert-Gourbeyre could identify 321 cases. The great majority were from Italy, France, Spain and Portugal, that is, from the major Roman Catholic countries. Sixty-two became "Saints", one-third of whom are Italian. Women outnumbered men by seven to one.

New Padre Pio

Ted Harrison's useful little book was published in 1994. It was probably already out-of-date for in a postscript he notes the death of a stigmatic he had only just interviewed. Harrison adds, that many stigmatics experience a time of depression and abandonment after the heights of their experience.

There seem to be about 10-15 major cases alive now, some of whom belong to nominally Protestant denominations. The youngest must be New Mexico evangelist Lucy Rael's daughter, who exhibited similar marks to her mother at only three weeks of age. Roberto Casavin, from near Rome, is being hailed as the "New Padre Pio". He will, no doubt, fill the void left by the fall of Virginia, alias Michele, Improta who was drawing hysterical crowds near Naples in the early 90's, that is, until unmasked as a transsexual fraud.

Stigmatics seem to be a mixed bag, some with highly impressionable minds, some unconscious masochists, some with bleeding tendencies enhanced by emotion and some simply fraudsters. It is notable that no cases occurred until about the year 1200, when Roman Catholic art began to produce harrowing pictures portraying bleeding wounds.

Stigmatics' wounds tend to match their local crucifix. If that has the nails through the palms, they have palm lesions; if through the wrists they have wrist lesions. They speak of their body wound being on the "correct" side, although Scripture does not actually specify a side. Again their wounds tend to match local crucifixes.

Rome is very wary of stigmatics as they can wield great influence, but Padre Pio's legacy could not be ignored. It is interesting to note that recently the *Catholic Times* has stressed Pio's obedience to the Church.

Christine Gallagher, a stigmatic of Western Ireland, gave her authority to the prophecy of a great "chastisement" before the year 2000, which, she says, her followers have the best chance of surviving.

If Padre Pio's followers are interested in signs, they might do well to ponder the fact that just as a crowd of 100,000 people were completing their vigil at San Giovanni on the occasion of the 30th anniversary of Padre Pio's death, an earthquake shook the region. Nobody was injured - at least not on this occasion!

CHAPTER FOUR

The Elusive Shadows of Opus Dei

The story of the detention of General Augusto Pinochet, the 83 year old former Chilean dictator, for human rights violations during his seventeen years in power, following the overthrow of Socialist President Salvador Allende in September 1973, has been widely covered in the secular and religious press.

According to Carlos Reyes of the anti-Pinochet *Chile Democratico*, "five priests and thousands of Catholics were put in prison and tortured and killed, and thousands more sent into exile during the Pinochet Years". However, the Pinochet affair has found Rome in an uncharacteristic state of diplomatic disarray, culminating in the disclosure on the 17th February 1999 by Baroness Symons of the Foreign Office, that there had been a formal approach from the Vatican, as long ago as last October, in support of Pinochet's safe return to Chile.

The Vatican v. Cardinal Hume

Channel 4 News was quick to pick up on the story and, under the provocative title *Christian Values*, commenced their item with the statement, "It's not very often the Vatican weighs in behind a man accused of crimes against humanity". It fell to Opus Dei member Dr. Joaquin Navarro-Valls, head of the Vatican Press Office, to confirm that the approach was official. Lord Lamont, who is Pro-Pinochet, then countered efforts to distance the Pope from this approach by stating firmly that such a diplomatic move could not take place without the Pontiff's approval. *The Times* reported the matter in greater depth on the 20th February under the headline *Catholic Church divided on Pinochet extradition*. The article went on to cover, in some detail, the internal divisions of the Church of Rome regarding this matter and, particularly, the embarrassment it must have caused Cardinal Hume. The Cardinal was already on record as saying to the BBC that people accused of acts such as those alleged of General Pinochet, "should be accountable for their actions".

Opus Dei v. Liberation Theology

This matter seems all the stranger to the Protestant onlooker because Latin America has been the setting for the massive Jesuit experiment of Liberation Theology. In one Latin American country after another the Jesuits have supported the under-classes in their attempts to over-throw the establishment, while consolidating and extending their own power under cover of the ensuing revolutionary confusion. However, in certain countries such as Columbia, Peru and Chile, experienced observers have detected another Roman policy directed at upholding reactionary right wing regimes, even in the face of the popular Liberation Catholicism. In countries where such a strategy is detectable it is notable that the shadowy and secretive organisation Opus Dei, although avowedly a non-political movement, happens to be strongly established. Hard facts are almost impossible to come by but allegations abound.

Right wing allegations

Professor Brian Smith of Massachusetts claimed in his book, *The Church and Politics in Chile*, 1989, published by the scholarly Princeton University Press, that Opus members "were among the first chief administrators of the brutally oppressive military regime of

General Pinochet". In December 1985, a Munich Court granted Opus Dei an injunction to prevent publication of another book in which it was alleged that certain Opus members had worked with the right wing Death Squads in Chile.

Further, the Latin American news sheet, *Noticias Aliadas* of 4th December 1975, alleged that Opus in Chile had begun to receive funds from conservative US foundations as early as 1962 to oppose the agrarian reforms of the then President Edwardo Frei. Bogota writer, Penny Lernoux, is on record as saying, "Opus Dei and *Fatherland and Liberty* (a right-wing terrorist group) worked together in Chile during the Allende years". In the American journal *Mother Jones*, for July 1983, Martin Lee claimed that "CIA money supported an Opus think tank, the Chilean Institute for General Studies". Opus Dei has always denied such accusations.

Opus v. Jesuits?

The Catholic historian, Michael Walsh, an ex-Jesuit and therefore potentially anti-Opus, makes an interesting comment in his popular biography of John Paul II. When the Pope visited Chile on the 1st April 1985, he was only the second Head of State to visit Pinochet at his residence. Walsh says pointedly that the visit took place, as archive footage from the time shows, at a time not only of considerable tension between the regime and the people and the regime and the Roman Catholic Church, but also between "the hierarchy and the more radical clergy working in the slum areas". Since Walsh is the author of the now dated but nevertheless valuable study *The Secret World of Opus Dei*, and a prominent authority on Opus Dei, one wonders whether one detects in his phraseology a reference to the confrontation between Opus influence among the hierarchy and Jesuit liberation influence on the streets - a tension within Rome which continues to this day and accounts for the Vatican's present diplomatic difficulties.

Walsh and Estruch

This raises the whole issue of how Protestants can obtain reliable information about Opus Dei. The internet carries a great deal of what appears to be official Opus information and also anti-Opus material, inserted by organisations set up to help disillusioned ex-members. The perennial problem of assessing the quality of internet information is heightened by the fact of Opus Dei's secrecy. However, the situation has been somewhat alleviated by the recent publication of an independent and authoritative study *Saints and Schemers* by Professor Joan Estruch of the Research Centre in Sociology of Religion. Elizabeth Ladd Glick's translation has been published by the prestigious Oxford University Press both here and in the United States. A careful comparison of Walsh with Estruch happily confirms the accuracy of Walsh.

The burning of the Carmelite Convent, Madrid 1931.

Furthermore, some of the material that Walsh gathered both from inside and outside Opus (and sometimes anonymously when concerned Romanists heard that he was writing an expose of that organisation) has been used as primary material in the Estruch study, thus demonstrating the regard in which it is held in academic circles.

Further confirmation of Walsh has followed with the publication by Opus of *Canonical Path*. This is an attempt to justify Opus' convoluted development in terms of Roman Canon Law. Opus has included in it a Latin Appendix of all the important documents in order to support its claim of legality - a claim which is obviously vital to an organisation professing to be an exemplar of Romish Orthodoxy. These documents were only available to Walsh through unofficial channels when he was writing. But, in the event, his rendering of them has been shown to be impeccably accurate.

The organisation

Thus, from the writings of Estruch and Walsh, we can be fairly certain that Opus Dei has about 80,000 members world wide. It is therefore approximately three times the size of the Society of Jesus. It has increased its membership by about 10,000 over the last 10 years. Opus Dei is, of course, Latin for 'The Work of God', but members often refer to it simply as 'The Work'. It is a hierarchical and militant association of some priests and a large number of laymen, usually from the highest echelons of society, who bring Opus immense influence, wealth and professional ability. This is reflected in its official title, "The Prelature of the Holy Cross and Opus Dei". The structure of Opus is a cause for concern to its opponents within Rome. This is because its leading prelate, who has always been a conservative Spaniard, has, since 1982, also been the spiritual director of the lay members throughout the world. The fear amongst non-Opus Romanists is that the authority and jurisdiction of the local Bishop is thereby usurped - something which the three leading Opus theologians (including Jose Louis Illanes, who was co-author of *Canonical Path*) have gone to great length to deny in their standard work on Opus practice (*Opus Dei in the Church*).

The role of the laity

The laymen are divided into three groups. The 'Numeries' remain celibate and live in an Opus Dei residence. They commit their entire salary to Opus Dei and submit all their incoming and outgoing mail to their directors. They follow a strict 'Plan of Life' involving daily Mass, Rosary, Opus prayers, cold showers, eating times and silence. They practice corporal mortification using a 'cilice', which is a spiked chain worn around the thigh and a 'Discipline', which is a knotted rope for whipping themselves.

'Supernumeries' are married and live with their families, but follow the *Plan of Life*, although usually ignorant of the Numery life.

'Supporters' or 'Co-operators' may not even be Roman Catholics but clearly could be of great use to the organisation for secretly penetrating societies, political systems and organisations, without their having any apparent link with Opus Dei. Much of Opus Dei recruitment goes on within Universities and it is quite usual for bright undergraduates, particularly in law, medicine or business to be approached at a time when they may be at their most idealistic and perhaps seeking to commit themselves more deeply to their Catholicism.

Origins of Opus

The 2nd October 1928 is a date greatly revered by Opus. It is set forth in all the official histories as the day on which the founder of Opus, Escriva Josemaria, in a Madrid Suburb, saw, by divine revelation, Opus in its final and completed form. Estruch has done much to confirm Walsh's suspicion that this is skilful re-writing of history. However, this date is so important to Opus Dei, that it even appears in the official Vatican personal prelature document of 1982 as "*... divina ductus inspiratione die II Octobris Anno MCMXXVIII...*" confirming the Vatican's belief that Opus is divinely inspired of God.

Escriva seems to have been an intelligent and restless man who could not settle with the humdrum life of being a parish priest. He was happiest when occupied in academic matters and pursuits connected with the teaching and guidance of students. The Estruch hypothesis of the origins of Opus Dei runs as follows. After the Spanish Civil War, there were a number of organisations about including some led by the Jesuits. The policy of General Franco's right wing regime was to re-establish the traditional link, often called "National Catholicism", between the Roman Catholic Church and the State. There was a great

The burning of the Jesuit Church and Headquarters, Madrid, 11ᵗʰ May, 1931.

need at this time for priests with Franco's outlook to join those of the Spanish intelligencia who held similar views.

The official histories seem to have taken great care to minimise what was probably a strong relationship between Escriva and Don Pedro Poveda, the Founder of the 'Institucion Teresiana', "whose goals and trajectory were quite similar to those of Opus Dei". Proveda was killed in the early days of the Civil War, thus leaving the field clear for Escriva.

Interestingly Estruch states that the 'Institucion Teresiana' sent its documents to the Vatican for Escriva beatification enquiries and never kept photocopies and they have now apparently disappeared.

Further, Escriva's original spiritual director had been a Jesuit. Escriva must have known of the "Associacion Catolica Nacional de Propagandistas", a continuation into business and professional life of devotional societies called "Sodalities of Our Lady", which were an Opus-like lay and clerical organisation under the direction of the Society of Jesus. This 'Association' had purchased a newspaper *El Debate* and Escriva worked in the School of Journalism attached to it during the Civil War.

Even within the emerging movement which was to become Opus Dei in post-Civil War Spain, there were other prominent men and one suspects that Escriva, partly by good fortune and partly because of his powerful, charismatic, intellectual personality, made himself the most prominent amongst a number of men of similar views in close fellowship. Walsh, for instance, describes a long time friendship with Isidoro Zorzano Ledesma, a distinguished engineer who died in July 1943, and whose canonisation was being pursued at one time, but was subsequently dropped to prepare the way for Escriva. Since this happened a long time before Escriva's death, it seems inconceivable that Escriva had nothing to do with it.

What seems particularly to have brought Escriva to the notice of the Franco Government is his association with Jose Maria Albareda Herrera, who was a good friend of Jose Ibanes Martin, Minister of Education from 1939 -1951. Herrera met Martin in Madrid during the Civil War period in the Chilean Embassy. Whether this is another elusive shadow of Opus Dei or just a sheer coincidence, one just cannot tell.

CHAPTER FIVE

Calvi's Ghost Still Haunts the Corridors of the Vatican

The body of Roberto Calvi, 'God's Banker', is to be exhumed in the course of a new enquiry, according to a report of 16 December 1998 in *The Times*, thus reminding us that the affair of Calvi and the Ambrosiano Bank is far from over.

New DNA evidence indicates that this international banker, found hanging under Blackfriars Bridge in 1982, may have been murdered rather than have taken his own life after the collapse of his financial empire with its intricate links with the Vatican. A sensational trial, with Mafia *pentiti* informing against their own, is likely to shake the Italian establishment later this year.

William Langley, with an eye no doubt to the topicality of the issue, recently interviewed Calvi's wife, Clara, in her Montreal home. The *Sunday Telegraph Magazine* illustrated Langley's article with a large picture of this forthright widow from whom *Assicurazioni Generalti* tried to deny a four billion lira pay out. Despite Langley's efforts to draw Clara on the scandals of Calvi, a "crook and a phoney" who undoubtedly "moved amongst thieves and liars", she simply reiterated her love from their first meeting and showed her enduring determination to prove that her husband was murdered.

Blackfriar's Bridge, London. Calvi's body was found hanging under the arches.

"The priests will kill you"

Clara's solemn look gives weight to a long held conviction concerning the Vatican and its priests. Langley reveals that Calvi had urged his wife to leave the Italy she clearly still loves should the need arise, reasoning, "If you stay behind the priests will kill you". At the time of his death she is on record as saying, "The Vatican had my husband killed to hide the bankruptcy of the Vatican bank". She has never forgotten that before his death he had told her, "The priests are going to make me pay for having brought up the name of the IOR (Vatican Bank). In fact, they are already making me pay". Amazingly this "crook and phoney" who moved amongst "thieves and liars", feared the priests more than all his other corrupt colleagues. He feared them more than Licio Gelli, the Venerable Grandmaster of the sinister *Propaganda Due* Masonic lodge to which any big businessman had to belong in the Italy of the seventies. He even feared the priests more than the Mafia who would undoubtedly want their money back or take revenge.

Whether the Mafia strung Calvi up or whether, in blind panic and despair, he took his own life, does not alter one fact. Across the almost unbelievable proportions of the crash of Calvi's Banco Ambrosiano and its empire, falls the shadow of the Vatican in the person of Archbishop Paul Casimir Marcincus, head of the IOR (the Vatican Bank). Whoever brought about Calvi's death, it had clearly been decided that Calvi was going to be the one 'to pay' and his testimony was going to be silenced.

Curiously the whole affair might never have happened if Marcincus had not been an 'outsider', unconnected by the traditional family ties, which have always united Popes and Bankers in a secure web of intrigue.

Banco di Santo Spirito

Anyone who wishes to conjure up in imagination the centuries of shady papal banking and business activities should take a walk along the ancient medieval pilgrimage route known as the *Via Coronari* or Street of the Rosary Sellers, where countless generations of pilgrims have purchased religious icons. This leads one to the *Banco di Santo*

Pope Alexander VII

Spirito, the bank of Pope Paul V, which stands on the site of the mint of Pope Julius II. Here during Reformation times, in the *Via del Banco di Santo Spirito*, at the foot of the Ponte St. Angelo, pilgrims could recharge their pockets and purses in readiness for a visit to the shrines of St. Peter's. An archway still exists which once led to the former business premises of Agostino Chigi, Il magnifico, of the Siennese banking dynasty, whose affairs were inseparable from those of the Vatican from the fourteenth to the nineteenth centuries. It was here that Chigi kept the pope's priceless, bejewelled, triple tiara, for many years, as security for a loan to Julius II. Interestingly Fabio Chigi, who became Pope Alexander VII, tried to dispense with the usual nepotistic appointments but as the Roman Catholic history *The Popes*, 1964 confirms, "He began by ... forbidding his relations to come to Rome; then, finding himself unable to do without them, brought a number of them from Sienna, made his nephew Flavio a Cardinal and gave lucrative offices to his brother and another nephew".

Again, in the 20th century, Pope Paul VI tried to avoid appointing his relations. He himself came from a banking background. Before becoming Pope he had for a while been Cardinal Archbishop of Milan - the city where Guiseppe Tovini had founded the greatly respected Catholic Banco Ambrosiano, for which he was beatified.

Papal nepotism

Paul VI came to the papal throne at the height of the Cold War and courted Moscow as much as Washington. He seems genuinely to have disliked the web of Pacelli nepotism he inherited from Eugenio Pacelli, the wartime Pius XII, who had his relations so closely involved with Vatican business, that it was commonly said of Italian companies, "If there is a Pacelli on the board, 6 to 4 it belongs to the Vatican".

Moreover, Vatican business had boomed after the war. This was helped by an extension of the already generous tax breaks of the 1929 Lateran treaty. By this concession, extracted from a preoccupied Mussolini on the 31st December 1924, Vatican share dividends were exempted from tax. This was good news for the Vatican Bank, the *Instituto per le Opere di Religione* or IOR. The IOR had only been set up, by revamping an existing obscure fund, on the 27th June previous, by Pius XII to finance good works such as the building of 'catholic' orphanages, a cause the CIA were anxious to further as the hedge against communism when the war ended.

This new fund, by the first of its six foundational clauses, was to be somewhat distanced from the oversight of the main Vatican financial department, the *L'Amministrazione del Patrimonio della Sede Apostolico* (A.S.P.A.). The ASPA, in its turn, had been set up in 1929 by the brother of the then Pope's closest cardinal friend. It had become vastly wealthy on ethic-free investment of the huge Lateran settlement, including gold.

Vatican brought to Court

When 'outsider' Paul VI ascended Peter's throne in the sixties the post-war boom was over. The Christian Democrat vote was falling and socialism gaining ground. To counter Pacelli nepotism and to further his Moscow credentials, Paul VI published, in 1967, the Encyclical *Populorum Progressivo* attacking laissez-fair Capitalism. Socialist pressure was demanding an end to the 1942 tax concession, which, although revoked in December 1962, was largely evaded until 1967 when arrears of 6.5 billion lira were owing. Vatican owned businesses were failing. Paul VI was terrified by the threat of angry redundant workers demonstrating outside their Vatican employer's H.Q. in St. Peter's Square. Further, the Vatican had to go to court to defend itself on charges of ill-advised and 'unscrupulous' property developments, of spoiling the Rome environment and of seeking to enhance the value of nearby Vatican owned land.

Paul VI won, but saw he had to act fast. The Vatican would divest itself of its loss making venture. This capital would be re-invested to gain a smaller stake in a much wider range of companies so that no Vatican representative would be needed for the board, thereby ensuring Vatican anonymity, should workers become restless. But, best of all, the Vatican would use its independent statehood to spirit lira to happier investment grounds abroad, blatantly flouting Italian law. The Vatican also helped good 'Catholic' Italian businessmen to do the same, for commission, creating the essential conditions for the Calvi fraud. The ailing companies were purchased by the Sicilian, Michele Sindona. (Sindona was ultimately jailed, following the fall of his fraudulent business empire, 'Il Crack Sindona'. He died in prison in March 1986 after drinking poisoned coffee).

Marcincus the outsider

To run the IOR Paul VI picked another 'outsider', an ambitious priest, the fifth child of Lithuanian immigrants in Chicago. He had no banking experience, and had become the Pope's protégé simply because he had on one occasion used his rugby player's physique to prevent the Pope being hurt in a crowd.

The best source of information about Marcincus is Raw's *The Money Changers* where the financial manipulations of the IOR are covered in detail. Raw worked primarily from documents and account sheets. He produces those most damaging to the IOR in an appendix. Raw was given exclusive access to the Calvi papers. He wisely fought shy of conspiracy theories and double interviewed witnesses to detect inconsistencies. This "long, detailed and complicated book" cites Marcincus at the outset as, "the crucial accomplice who made the fraud possible" and after 500 pages of factual proof concludes that "He (Marcincus) is the most prominent of Calvi's associates to have escaped judicial condemnation". Marcincus remained a prisoner within the confines of the Vatican State until 1ᵗʰ July 1987, when the Pope's lawyers, in the Italian Supreme Court of Appeal, succeeded in reversing an earlier decision of the court that Italian State Warrants were valid in papal territory. Marcincus retired quietly to the USA in 1990, still protesting his innocence. He failed to fulfil the forecast of experienced Vatican watcher, Nino Lo Bello, made in the 70's, that Marcincus was " a sure bet to be a cardinal before the decade is out ... with a good chance of being the first American Pope ever". The trouble with Marcincus was that he was an 'outsider'.

Eventually, in 1984, eighty-eight creditor banks forced the Vatican to pay over $250,000,000. How the Vatican covered its losses, to say nothing of securing a discount for immediate settlement, is still unclear. The contrived and extraordinary Holy Year of 1983, the sale of temporary rights to Nippon TV, for the filming of Sistine Chapel art, and the opening of the fabulous Vatican library (which ironically was originally the Chigi collection) for fine facsimiles, will have helped.

However, Rome is far-sighted. It is probably no coincidence that the settlement of the New Concordat on 26th January 1984 was followed only months later by the sudden Ambrosiano settlement, after prolonged prevarication. The Christian Democratic vote was at an all time low and the left of the then Craxi coalition were crying out for a reduction of Rome's grip on the Italian state with a re-negotiated Concordat. At the same time, the right were demanding more state funding of priest's stipends.

The Vatican would have realised that Craxi had to obtain a prompt settlement of the Ambrosiano affair. Craxi would understand that Concordat terms in the Vatican's favour would assist in securing the Vatican's co-operation in kindly making its 'voluntary contribution' to the Ambrosiano creditors in exchange for enduring legal immunity. To this day Rome refuses to acknowledge guilt.

Whether the traditional Vatican financial network is now securely reinstated we may soon discover.

How Calvi and the Vatican Worked the Fraud

At the risk of over-simplification, it can be said that the fraud was based on the fact that the Calvi empire was divided into three parts.

First there was the Italian Banco Ambrosiano and its subsidiaries.

Second were the legitimate off-shore Ambrosiano Banks, especially the Cisalpine in Nassau. Thirdly there was Calvi's secret network of "Brass Plate" companies with no physical presence.

The basic mechanism of the fraud was a so-called *in conto deposito* or "back to back" operation which worked like this. The Ambrosiano Bank deposited Italian Lira in the Vatican Bank (the IOR), which changed them into foreign currency, and sent them abroad to the Cisalpine Bank and elsewhere. The deposits returned from overseas were similarly handled by the IOR, the Vatican earning commission on each transaction. This enabled Calvi to get round the extremely stringent Italian State currency regulations. It also freed the transactions from prying eyes of accountants and auditors.

However, these returning deposits from the Cisalpine were paid, not into the legitimate Italian Banco Ambrosiano, but into the accounts of the secret network of "Brass Plate" companies, held at the Banca Gottardo in Switzerland. From here Calvi decided whether the money went to Gelli, to the Mafia or back into other enterprises such as purchasing Ambrosiano shares at inflated prices thereby pushing up the value of the bank and his own profile as a loan-worthy banker.

That the IOR assisted Calvi in passing money to Gelli was proven by a *tabella*, or account, actually found in Gelli's possession when he was arrested in Geneva on 13th September 1981.

Marcincus was a Director of the Nassau Cisalpine from 1971 and regularly saw Calvi at board meetings. By 1981 Marcincus realised that a burgeoning black hole was appearing in the Calvi empire.

Instead of denouncing the fraud, Marcincus issued Calvi with "letters of patronage" signed by himself on IOR paper on the 1st of September 1981, allowing the good financial standing of the Vatican to vouchsafe for Calvi's ailing companies, thereby falsely allaying the fears of Calvi's chief executives.

However, the "patronage letters" were only issued after Calvi had been forced to sign a letter of indemnity on 26th August 1981, on overseas headed paper, absolving the IOR of all consequences of issuing the patronage letters and stipulating "elimination" of the IOR's involvement in these operations by 30th June 1982.

This drove Calvi into a frenzy of ill advised banking activities, which was clearly unsustainable and inevitably brought about the collapse of his business empire. Marcincus had effectively placed the noose around Calvi's neck.

CHAPTER SIX

Pope Joan - An Important 'Dialogue' Reopened

When one comes across a quaint old Protestant book dealing with an ancient scandal of the papacy, one should always look carefully at the date of publication. In all probability the author was trying to counter a fresh assault by the church of Rome at that time. Thus an old yellowed quarto in the writer's possession, *"Pope Joane A Dialogue between a Protestant and a Papist - Manifestly proving a woman called Joane was Pope of Rome: against the surmises and objections made to the contrary by Robert Bellarmine and Caesar Baronius Cardinals: Florimundus Raemondus, N.D. and other popish writers impudently denying the same"* was not published without design in 1625. Our nation at that time needed to understand the implications of the papacy of Joan. Hence the author's earnest Epistle Dedicatory to Tobias Archbishop of York "that by your Grace's means the Epha, wherein Popish wickedness sitteth may be lift up ... and carried out".

For 1625 was the year of the accession of Charles I to the throne and some clergy were abandoning their former Protestant stance to accommodate Charles Romeward sympathies. Only two years previously Charles had made a secret visit to Spain "in order to conclude a marriage treaty with the daughter of King Philip III". He had refused openly to convert to Catholicism, no doubt because he wanted to retain his throne. But the warning was plain. Protestantism was in danger, a presentiment fully born out by subsequent events.

Bellarmine and Baronius

Alexander Cooke, the author of the "dialogue" explains his reason for presenting his argument in this form in a preface addressed "To the Popish or Catholicke Reader". These reasons are "that I might meet more fully the cavils which thy proctors use in pleading of this case: and that it might be better understood of Common Readers who are sooner gulled with continued discourses". One may be sure that such "discourses" were numerous and the matter a weighty one if Rome chose to employ Bellarmine and Baronius, the two great apologists of the Counter Reformation, to refute it.

The Dialogue opens thus:

Protestant. "Well met and welcome home Sir. What new booke have you brought us downe from London this Mart?"

Papist. "I have an excellent booke, which discouseth at large about Pope Joan, whose Popedom you cast in the Catholicke's teeth so often".

Interestingly, the same Dialogue has been reopened recently with the publication of *The She Pope: A Quest for the Truth behind the mystery of Pope Joan* (Heinemann 1998) by Peter Stanford, former editor of the *Catholic Herald*. Clearly this matter is still a great embarrassment to Rome.

High amongst the Papal Claims and essential to the power and prestige of the Papacy is the Apostolic Succession. Zacchello has written an excellent book demolishing the Romish position in which he explains Rome's doctrine as follows: Christ gave the power of the keys to Peter, but not to the others "indicating supreme authority" so that "By legitimate succession the one that succeeded as Bishop of Rome after Peter's death inherited the office as head of the Church". Rome points to her list of Popes whose orderly succession from Peter she regards as miraculous. She brushes aside the many gaps in the list which she blames on the inevitable inaccuracies of record keeping in the Dark Ages. However, should there have been without doubt a female Pope, one of the main pillars of the Papal edifice is demolished for ever.

Pope Joan

The story of Pope Joan concerns an Englishwoman in the 9th century who, disguised as a man, gained the papal chair by deception as John VIII, only to be unmasked some years later by giving birth in the midst

Woodcut of Pope Joan.

The 'Vicus Papissa' or 'Street of the Woman Pope', The Edicola (Shrine) probably marks the spot where her statue, confirmed by early travellers, stood. It may be where she gave birth. The Popes will not go down this street.

of a public papal procession. A shrine still marks this spot on the ancient processional route between the Coliseum and St. John Lateran. A 14th century French miniature was reproduced in an article by Stanford promoting his book in the *Sunday Telegraph Magazine* of April 5th 1998. This shows a woman wearing the triple crown and papal vestments with a new born baby appearing from beneath them, proving that at an early stage the story was widely known.

Stanford reveals that Rome still clings to the defence current in 1625, when Cooke wrote the Dialogue. For, says Stanford, "the standard Catholic response to this tale" is still "to dismiss it as a Post-Reformation Protestant plot to disgrace the Papacy". The Reformers are indicted with illegally entering Catholic libraries and falsifying papal records. Happily, Stanford is able to testify that his privileged inspection of the Bodleian copy of Dominican Martin of Poland's *Chronicle of Popes and Emperors*, published in 1277, which is one of the important pieces of evidence for Joan's existence, shows no trace of such vandalism in this country, where such interference would have been most easily effected.

Emmanuel Rhoidis

The best and most easily obtained Protestant defence of the truth of the story of Pope Joan is the Alexander Ratcliffe reprint of the summary of the evidence by Emmanuel Rhoidis. It is a translation from the Greek by the great Victorian Protestant Charles Hastings Collette at the end of the 19th century, and is unanswerable. Collette undertook the translation for just the same reason that Cooke published his dialogue, namely to oppose the serious increase in Romanist influence in our land at the time. To my mind one of Rhoidis most convincing arguments is that when John Huss, the Bohemian Reformer, was on trial for his life at Constance, accused of heresy, he referred four times to Pope Joan destroying the claim to apostolic succession. This was before an audience representing the cream of the learning of the age. Yet "not one of the 20 cardinals, not one of the 49 bishops, not one of the 272 theologians, charged him with lying or uttering a blasphemy with his statement".

Sedia Stercoraria

There is also the matter of the *sedia stercoraria* used in past papal coronations. In Mendham's *Life of Pius V* (1566-1572), based on the records of eye-witnesses, he describes the scene at the Lateran: "The Pope is led by the prior and canons to the marble chair, situated before the principal door on the left, called the *sedes stercorarias* where he sits, *so as to seem rather to lie*" (italics in the original). Whilst in this extraordinary position I Samuel 2:8 is read: "He raiseth the poor out of the dust and lifteth up the beggar from the dunghill, to set them among princes and to inherit the throne of glory". In Latin dunghill is translated *stercora* and this allusion has remained for centuries the official explanation of this ritual.

Stanford found an old engraving of Innocent X on the *sedia stecoraria*, the backtilted papal throne, used at the election of the popes for centuries, with an acolyte examining him and announcing that he is a man. So Stanford went in search of the chair.

He was given access to a private part of the Vatican museum and found just such a chair, and despite protestations that this was an ancient commode, he came away convinced it was the *sedia stercoraria* mentioned so frequently in descriptions of papal coronations, and apparently specifically linked to the matter of Pope Joan by Platina the scholarly librarian of Sixtus IV (1471-1484) in his revered *Lives of the Popes*. How else could Rome explain the sexing of popes before they finally mounted St. Peter's throne, except by the fear that another female should gain the position by deception?

So the ancient 'dialogue' can and must be reopened.

CHAPTER SEVEN

John Paul II's Nationalism and Attempts to Placate the Jews

"When he was still Bishop of Krakow, Karol Wojtyla (now Pope John Paul II) said in 1972 that the Shoah (the Holocaust) was an expiatory sacrifice which the Jews had to make to be forgiven for the death of Jesus and that Auschwitz was their Golgotha". (*Le Monde* 20th March 98).

The Vatican spokesman Joaquin Navarro-Valls, a member of Opus Dei, has naturally denied this statement "strenuously".

However, Rome remains as insensitive as ever to Jewish feelings. The *Catholic Times* of 22nd August 1999 was constrained to print a letter by Geoffrey D. Paul, former editor of the *Jewish Chronicle*, complaining about an article entitled, *The anti-Semitic legacy* by Fr. Francis Marsden, a regular columnist in the *Catholic Times*. The article had clearly given offence despite Fr. Marsden's attempts, as he thought, to be constructive.

Attempts at reconciliation

The present Pope set himself to heal the rift with the Jews. On 13th of April 1986 he came "to listen" in the Rome synagogue which is situated in the former ghetto. He told Chief Rabbi Elio Toaff, "We have a relationship with his faith as with no other. Judaism is not separate - you are our favoured brothers and it could be said our elder brethren".

We Remember is Rome's apology for the holocaust. It was written to "heal the wounds of past injustices". In the Pope's personal endorsement of this document he calls the holocaust an "indelible stain" and an "unspeakable iniquity".

Yet on 25th June 1987, a year after his synagogue visit and just before an important meeting with Jewish leaders in Miami planned for 11th September, the Pope officially received Kurt Waldheim, President of Austria, in the Vatican, whilst an Austrian commission (to which Waldheim was widely believed to have lied) was actually investigating Waldheim's part in the deportation of Greek Jews in World War II. It was only a few weeks earlier that the pope had visited the extermination camp at Majdanek near Lublin, a principle destination for the Greek Jews.

A frantic damage limitation exercise followed, with a hastily arranged meeting at Castel Gandolfo on 1st September, involving Cardinal Willebrands and the international Jewish Committee for Inter-religious Affairs.

Provocative canonisations

Since then the Jews have been offered further provocations. The Pope was the chief mover behind the hasty beatification of Escriva, the founder of Opus Dei in May 1992 amidst headlines such as, "Opus Dei denies Hitler claims" (*Universe* 19th January). Escriva was accused of anti-Semitism, of contemplating sending members of his order as recruits to the German army and of denying the extent of the holocaust, declaring that, "Certainly there were no more than three or four million Jews exterminated".

Moreover, the Vatican has continued to push for the beatification of Pius XII who remained silent about the treatment of the Jews in the last war. His beatification was criticised by the conservative BBC 2 series *Reputations* as far back as 1995.

Then Elam Steinberg, General Secretary of The World Jewish Congress, alleged in 1998 that the Vatican had benefited from Jewish gold looted in World War II. The Vatican absolutely denied both this and the possibility that archive material might exist to settle the matter.

We Remember continued to excuse Pius XII's role in the war. In June a papal visit to Austria produced another warm handshake for Waldheim. On 3rd October the Pope beatified Cardinal Alojzije Stepinac, who had co-operated with Hitler through the fascist Ustashi regime in Croatia. A week later the Pope canonised Edith Stein, a Jewish philosopher, who converted to Roman Catholicism, became a nun and was martyred in Auschwitz.

St. Edith Stein

The Edith Stein affair caused uproar amongst Jewish people who maintain that she was martyred for her Jewish origins and not her Romanism. The Vatican stuck to its claim. The headline in *L'Osservatore* (the official Vatican Newspaper) of 14th October ran: "Edith Stein's sole boast was the Cross of our Lord Jesus Christ".

John Paul II said at the canonisation ceremony: "The value of her testimony is to render ever more solid the bridge of mutual under-standing between Christians and Jews". But the canonisation was reported by Jewish groups as "a slap in the face" for Holocaust victims. They made it quite clear that they still regarded the issue of Rome's "complicity" in the murder of Edith Stein as unresolved. Daniel Farhi of the French Jewish Liberal Movement said that the canonisation would inflict "a fresh wound in the hearts of [holocaust] victim's descendants". The Simon Wiesenthal Centre called it "outrageous" and commented that the pope clearly thought the best Jews were those who become Roman Catholic converts!

Auschwitz

Auschwitz is central to understanding John Paul II. He was born at Wadowice, a few miles from Aswiecim, an industrial town less than 50 miles west of Krakow, Poland's ancient capital. Aswiecim was renamed Auschwitz when the Nazi's set up a concentration camp there in 1940. Both Jews and Gentiles were incarcerated and over 50% of these were Polish citizens.

The nationalist sentiments of gentile Poles (and therefore of this pope) are rooted in the virulent Catholicism of the Counter-Reformation. They recall that a fifth of the Polish nation perished in World War II and regard the site of Auschwitz as a national Catholic shrine.

As the Nazi 'Final Solution' escalated, so Auschwitz became too small for their purpose and the railway was extended three kilometres to Brzezinka, known as Birkenau by the Germans. It was here at this larger site that the bulk of the Jewish extermination occurred. (Nearly two million people perished in the two camps, of which 90% were Jewish).

Birkenau was flattened after the war and the Communists created a museum at Auschwitz. Information was presented in conformity with Russian Communist dogma. Polish children were usually shown only Auschwitz as Birkenau was less interesting and more remote. Omission of the Jewish perspective at Auschwitz by the Communists paved the way for the Roman Catholic Church after the fall of communism to subordinate the obvious prior Jewish claim to the site to Polish nationalist Roman Catholic culture.

Polish Monks and Nuns going to the Lateran for mass.

The crucifix war

In 1984, during the Lech Walesa Solidarity era, when Rome was challenging Communism and John Paul II was now the symbol of

Polish cultural identity, a Carmelite convent was established against the walls of Auschwitz concentration camp in a building where the poison gas Zyklon B was formerly stored. The nuns were inspired by hagiographies of the Auschwitz martyrs Maximilian Kolbe and Edith Stein. Crosses began to appear on the site. The World Jewish Congress complained and in 1987 Rome agreed that the convent should go. The nuns prevaricated. Jewish activists from the USA and Israel staged prolonged protests. On July 14th 1989 Rabbi Weiss was filmed being drenched with what he claimed to be water mixed with urine and faeces thrown from the upper windows. He was forcibly dragged away while the nuns watched and a priest shouted abuse. Rabbi Weiss later called this an "echo of what was 50 years ago".

The threat of a Jewish boycott of the 50th anniversary of the Warsaw ghetto uprising finally saw the nuns relocated one km south west of Auschwitz in a convent next to an Information, Dialogue and Prayer Centre. The crucifixes, however, remained and indeed grew in number.

The 50th anniversary celebrations of the liberation of Auschwitz saw another front page disaster for Rome's relations with the Jews as they arranged their own official celebrations a day earlier. Walesa was forced to tone down the nationalism of his prepared speech before the world's leaders. And Rabbi Weiss was once more forcibly ejected.

The crucifix war has continued to rage with the *Catholic Times* risking giving offence with headlines such as: "Auschwitz - Does it really need to be so ugly?" This was illustrated with pictures of Polish activists planting even more crosses. At last, in June of this year (1999), despite threats by Polish nationalists to blow up the site, the police began to implement new legislation enforcing a 100 metre protected zone around the camp. The crosses have now been removed, that is, except for the 26 foot cross erected in 1979 after John Paul's first Auschwitz mass as pontiff.

The Pope at Auschwitz

John Paul II's agenda, which his biographers call his zeal to "incorporate every reality ... into his Christian - Polish vision", is now pursued with greater circumspection. But in that heady first year of his pontificate he knew nothing of such reserve. On 7th June 1979 he arrived at Auschwitz in the afternoon sunshine fresh from a triumphant visit to his neighbouring birthplace of Wadowice. Surely, his childhood there, growing up amongst liberal Jews, living in one of their rented properties, playing football with his best friend, the Jewish Jerzy (Jurek) Kluger, meant that by God's providence the best man possible was now ready to bring about reconciliation with that race? In the event his words at Auschwitz betrayed only his ethnic blindness.

The Pope's entourage of cardinals, bishops, nuns and girls in white first communion dresses clutching colourful bunches of flowers, heard

him wax long on the merits of Kolbe, his childhood hero, who was also born nearby, and Stein. He then termed the camp, "this special shrine, the birthplace I can say [which was actually rather stretching the truth] of St. Stanislaus, Patron of the Poles". Much more followed about the site

Numerous Polish tourists buses

being an international war monument. He briefly mentioned the Jews, only to pass on immediately to the matter of the six million Poles who had perished in "the centuries old fight of this nation, my nation, for its fundamental rights among the people of Europe".

Thus, at a stroke, he had denied the unique role of Auschwitz in the Jewish holocaust, removed it from the domain of the international community and given it to the Poles as a symbol of nationhood in their struggle against Germany and Russia. He had inaugurated decades of conflict with the Jews, which shows no signs of abating. Indeed, the widely rumoured decision of John Paul to be buried - against all precedent in Poland, could well serve to prolong this quarrel for generations. For Pope John Paul, former Archbishop of Krakow, whose relics are already accumulating at Wadowice, would almost certainly want his final resting place to be where it would for ever associate his name with Auschwitz.

CHAPTER EIGHT

Murder in the Vatican

It is always a relief to come out into the Italian sunshine after visiting the temples of Rome, and it was never more so than after a recent visit to the newly refurbished St. Peter's. The Monument to Pius XII, Eugenio Pacelli, the pope of World War II, accused of anti-Semitism, is always macabre, but his gaunt and pitiless features are particularly evident on sunny days.

I was reminded of it when I saw one of the more recent Jesuit defences of Pius XII, entitled *Pio XII e la Seconda Guerra Mondiale*, by Fr. Pierre Blet, prominently displayed in the bookshop opposite the Gregorian University. The cream of the next generation of priests and nuns stream out of the "Greg" at midday and many go straight to the bookshop opposite, where they cannot help but see the book.

The Scripture came to mind, "How long O Lord, holy and true, dost thou not judge and avenge". Then I found myself reading the front page of *La Repubblica*, one of the main Italian dailies. The headlines ran "Pio XII non sara tra i beati del Duemila", declaring that Pius XII will not be beatified before the millennium. The reporter, Gad Lerner, went on to explain that Pope John Paul II cannot risk such a controversial beatification because he is planning to use the millennium both as an ecumenical opportunity and to further inter-religious dialogue.

The Vatican's change in strategy, which is probably only a postponement, must be at least partly a consequence of the enormous publicity surrounding John Cornwell's book *Hitler's Pope: the Secret History of Pius XII.*

'The Church is in Uproar'

Cornwell is a journalist who described himself as a "practising Catholic and seminarian". His book has caused a stir because, as the *Sunday Times* of 12th September 1999 observed, "Cornwell set out to defend the controversial wartime Pope, Pius XII, against charges of anti-Semitism. But a shock awaited him at the Vatican. Now Rome is trying to hide the truth and the church is in uproar".

Pius XII was surrounded by Jesuits and his beatification is their particular cause. A senior Jesuit, Dr. Peter Gumpel, "took a great risk", so we are told, by allowing Cornwell access both to the Jesuit's own canonisation archives and also to certain hitherto secret material in the Vatican. This gamble on behalf of the "beautiful, saintly" Pacelli, as Jesuit Gumpel describes him, was no doubt intended to clinch Pius' beatification in the year 2000.

The world HQ of the Society of Jesus.

When Gumpel realised that his scheme had backfired, he telephoned Cornwell at Jesus College, Cambridge, threatening him with legal action. His "anger and dismay" were no doubt compounded by the prospect of what *Repubblica* hints will be a ceremony of unparalleled splendour to canonise, in Pius XII place, Popes John XXIII and Paul VI, whose names are suddenly cropping up in the Catholic press. What is more, the present Pope will once again have snubbed the Jesuits.

Too credible

Cornwell is a former student of Oscott College, where Cardinal Newman was received after his defection to Rome. The Jesuits chose him because of his former services to the papacy in trying to combat the report that John Paul II's predecessor, John Paul I, had been murdered by poisoning in 1978. The Vatican was particularly worried about the book *In God's Name* by David Yallop, published in 1984. The trouble with Yallop's account was that it was so credible. Yallop had been brought up a Roman Catholic, but left the Roman church at the age of 15, because the recently propounded Dogma of the Assumption insulted his intelligence. Yallop's book has now sold over five million copies and is widely known in Protestant circles. It still sells well in Rome under the title *In Nome di Dio*. So in 1987 the Jesuits gave Cornwell the job of refuting it.

The Miraculous and Demonic

The Jesuits were actually at that time assisting Cornwell to research yet another book he was writing which dealt with the miraculous and demonic in Roman Catholicism. No doubt they were hoping that Cornwell would authenticate the increasingly popular Marian apparitions at Medjugorje. Jesuit Father Richard Foley was an enthusiast for these apparitions which the Vatican was refusing to recognise.

So Cornwell came to Rome to get "official ecclesiastical answers" about Medjugorje. His visit coincided with the Vatican's realisation that the Yallop account of the cause of Pope John I's death was being widely accepted. Rome needed "unprecedented" help with this

Tomb of John Paul II in the Vatican Grottoes.

matter which was far more pressing than the Marian apparitions at Medjugorje. So they recruited Cornwell. He recalls being "suddenly and surprisingly encouraged" and given a formal blessing by Archbishop John Foley of the Vatican media office to consider a quite different project. ... The Vatican expected me to prove that John Paul I had not been poisoned by one of their own." The Archbishop promised that the Vatican would be "opened up" for Cornwell.

Thief in the Night

Yallop's conclusion had been, "The decision that the Pope must die was taken and God's Candidate [John Paul I] was murdered". Cornwell's reply, entitled *A Thief in The Night*, concluded that: "John Paul I died scorned and neglected by the institution that existed to sustain him". Another journalist summarised Cornwell's conclusions as: "John Paul I was not murdered so much as allowed to die for want of medical care, denied an autopsy for reasons that remain mysterious, and buried with a death certificate which in England or America, would not have been legal". From all this it is clear that Cornwell found much to arouse his suspicions about John Paul I's death, but fell just short of the conclusion that he was murdered by digitalis poisoning. This makes Cornwell's recent change of mind about Pacelli all the more interesting. Had Cornwell known then what he knows now about the ways of the Vatican, he might have come to the conclusion that John Paul I was poisoned after all.

Moral shock

Let us return to Pius XII. Cornwell wrote in the *Sunday Times* article, "I always believed Pacelli was innocent. I could not imagine that a pope of such evident holiness could be guilty of silent complicity in the holocaust and I originally set out to write a definitive book in his defence. ... After reading through the combined archives alongside a huge amount of historical scholarship on Vatican Diplomacy in Germany in the 1920s and 1930s, I found myself in moral shock. The material I had gathered, taking the more extensive view of Pacelli's life, amounted not to an exoneration but to a wider indictment". If Cornwell had written *A Thief in the Night* with his present insights into the workings of the Vatican, might he not have taken Yallop's explanation of John Paul I's death more seriously?

In 1989 Cornwell said he had "an open mind" when he wrote the refutation of Yallop's thesis and he promised ruthless exposure of any shred of evidence indicating poisoning. But he also said, "I was not easily inclined to believe that senior prelates in the church had conspired ... in a plot to kill John Paul I". And at the outset of his investigation, he described Yallop's book as "scandalous". So his mind was not that open.

It is therefore of interest briefly to reconsider the facts. John Paul I died on 28th September 1978. Yallop published his book in 1984, "the product of three years research", much of it clandestine. Cornwell, on the other hand, did not publish his refutation until 1989 and that after only two years of largely Vatican facilitated research. When Yallop and Cornwell met on 6th January 1988 ,Yallop, recalling his own experience, told Cornwell:

"You're dealing with people who are lying to you ... they are duplicitous men". Passage of time could only confirm this objection. For example, in a unique interview with Marcinkus, the Vatican banker, Cornwell found Marcinkus launching at once into his disputed alibi and "leading the interview".

What Yallop described was a mafia style murder with the "morticians ordered before a body is found". Yallop claimed that the Vatican delayed the announcement until the murder scene had been tidied up. A nun, Sister Vincenza, had served the pope coffee at 4.30 am for 18 years. She therefore raised the alarm by about 4.45 am. The official Vatican statement ran: "This morning, September 29th, 1978, about 5.30, the private Secretary to the Pope ... found him dead in bed with the light on". Cornwell confirmed that the Vatican had lied over who discovered the pope, but affirmed the 5.30 timing, despite knowing that Sr. Vincenza, who had since died, personally told Yallop, at interview it was 4.30.

Signoracci brothers

ANSA, a reputable Italian news agency, put out a report at 7.43 am concerning the summoning of the morticians. "Two of the Signoracci brothers ... were woken up this morning at dawn and at 5 o'clock were collected by a Vatican car ...". The journalist Mario de Francesco, who wrote this was traced and he confirmed the accuracy of the report to Yallop and later Cornwell. De Francesco's source was the papal mortician brothers themselves, who, incidentally, were paid nothing for their services except medals making them Knights of Gregory. Maybe, the morticians could not be trusted when Yallop's researcher triple interviewed them, let alone when Cornwell eventually met them. But why should they have lied or got confused on the day of the death, before much controversy had yet arisen, and events were fresh in their minds? They were only asked a simple question and they had no reason to lie.

Cardinal Thomas Winning in a recent attack on Cornwell's *Hitler's Pope* made an interesting remark. It confirmed my own observation as soon as I received my own copy and turned to the bibliography. Cardinal Winning said, "With a few exceptions, Mr. Cornwell confines himself to secondary sources ..." In fact Cornwell's use of the *Teste* or Canonisation file of the Jesuits is quite limited. It is as though this opened his eyes to see the truth already clear in the documents long available in the public domain. Anyone who carefully reads Hebrew historian Saul Friedlander's *Pius XII and the Third Reich, A Documentation* in 1966, could not have failed to see Pius' guilt then, even though the book was based on the German archives alone. Friedlander, whose parents were killed at Auschwitz, tried in those days "several times to get access to the Vatican archives, but in vain".

Subsequent Vatican archive revelations have only provided additional confirmation of Pius' guilt. In the light of what Cornwell learnt of the Vatican's methods when researching *Hitler's Pope*, one wonders what Cornwell's conclusion would be if he were to re-investigate John Paul I's death now.

Cornwell's *A Thief in the Night* does however provide an alternative for people who dislike conspiracy theories. Cornwell had never heard "of any pope in living memory referred to by the Catholic clergy in such a slighting way". John Paul I was described to him as "out of his depth ... everybody knew it ... he just couldn't cope ... they've made Peter Sellers a pope ... a gauche and incompetent figure of fun". He also describes the petty rivalries and jealousies of those in intermediate positions in the Vatican. Frustrated by celibacy and destined never to reach the most senior posts, they satisfy their ambition by association with the charismatic men who do. Perhaps they saw the prestige of their masters threatened and by implication their own. Who could be better placed then they to remove such an embarrassing occupant of the papal chair?

CHAPTER NINE

Rome's Holy and Prestigious Face: The Turin Shroud

Ian Wilson has argued for the genuineness of the Turin Shroud all his life. Yet by 1991 when his book *Holy Faces Secret Places* appeared the shroud had already been proved to be a mediaeval forgery.

The linen cloth purports of course to be the one in which Joseph of Arimathea wrapped the body of Jesus (Matthew 27:59). A sample was removed on 21 April 1988 for carbon dating by leading scientists at three independent centres in Switzerland, England and the USA.

The results were what most Protestants would have anticipated. On 13 October 1988 the respected co-ordinator of the venture, Dr. Michael Tite, held a press conference in the British Museum, where he worked. The result of the investigations were written starkly on the blackboard: "1260-1390".

Nature

The following year the leading scientific journal *Nature* (Feb. 1989) commented: "These results therefore provide conclusive evidence that the linen of the Shroud of Turin is Mediaeval". Professor Hall of the Oxford team put it more bluntly, "Someone just got a bit of linen, faked it and flogged it".

In those dark days Wilson wrote, "All the hitherto, arguably compulsive, amalgam of knowledge suggestive of the shroud's authenticity" has been "blown sky high".

However, Wilson has clearly recovered and published a new book *The Blood and the Shroud*, which has been arranged, with great good sense and business acumen, to coincide with this year's public exposition of the icon from 18 April to 14 June. (His original book *The Turin Shroud* was also published at the time of a public showing, in 1978, when three million people made the pilgrimage). In his new book Wilson attempts a defence along two lines.

Bioplastic coating and pollens

First he questions the carbon dating by suggesting that the fibres of the shroud had become covered, as old objects do, with a 'bioplastic coating' which was not removed. He claims that this could give a carbon-14 dating error of a thousand years.

When Professor Hall was interviewed on ITV earlier this year he said, with evident irritation in his voice, "Nothing has changed. There is no further evidence that the shroud is earlier than mediaeval".

Wilson's second line is to try to strengthen the historical links between Jerusalem of AD 33 and the sudden appearance of the shroud at Lirey in France where it was first shown in 1357 (a date which fits nicely within the C-14 estimate of 1260-1390). He quotes Max Frei, a Professor of Botany, who states that the pollens on the shroud fit species local only to its alleged journey from Jerusalem via Edessa and Constantinople. Even so, Sheldon Grossman reviewing the book for the *Catholic Herald* (May 24) describes Wilson's arguments as 'somewhat forced'.

Jesuit Thurston

A hundred years ago an influential Jesuit, Herbert Thurston, wrote that "it is highly probable an artist used a model" to paint it in mediaeval times. "Why should it have retained its brilliance through countless journeys and changes of climate for 15 centuries" unless "it be a fabrication?"

So why does Rome expect another three million pilgrims this year and more for the year 2000, if there is so much scepticism within her own ranks? The answer must lie in her rejection of Bible Christianity.

"They received not the love of the truth that they might be saved. And for this cause God shall send them strong delusion, that they should believe a lie" (II Thess. 2:10,11), making them unable to see through deceitful priestcraft which entices pilgrims, who are anxious to be right with

19th Century exposition. Turin Shroud with markings clearer than today.

God, to strive for extravagant indulgences (see *English Churchman* 8 May 1998 p.5).

Surprisingly, even Roman Catholic voices have protested against the "immaturity" and "semi-paganism" of the hysteria surrounding the current exposition (*The Universe* 3 May p.10). Toll free phone lines have been advertised throughout Roman Catholic Europe to reserve standing space for the timid. In the Dark Ages it was not unusual for pilgrims to be trampled to death in the rush to get a closer look at one of the numerous shrouds in Christendom.

The dean's avarice

In fact an account of this hysteria provides the strongest evidence regarding the forger and for the C-14 dating.

There exists in the French archives copies of a letter from the Bishop of Troyes to the then Pope Clement VII. It reads: "The case Holy Father stands thus. For some time since, in this diocese of Troyes, the Dean of a certain collegiate church, to wit that of Lirey, falsely and deceitfully, being consumed with the passion of avarice ... procured for his church a certain cloth cunningly painted, upon which ... was depicted the twofold image of one man ... [the dean] falsely declaring this was the actual shroud in which our Saviour was enfolded in the tomb ... The story was put about ... throughout the world ... and so that the money might be wrung out of [pilgrims] pretended miracles were worked". The resulting stampede to Lirey caused "prudent persons to take action ... Eventually ... the truth was attested to by the artist who painted it". The dean, however, "hid away the said cloth", thus assuring the perpetuation of the fraud.

Engraving of 1703 Exposition of the Turin Shroud.

Duke Emmanuel Philibert

The circumstances of the shroud coming to Turin also involved prestige and avarice. The Dukes of Savoy, the tyrannical persecutors of the Waldensian Protestants, having been forced by the French to reduce their territories, attempted to glorify their new capital, Turin. When in 1578 the reverend Bishop of Milan, Charles Borromeo, expressed his desire to make a barefoot pilgrimage to the shroud, which was then at Chamberey, as a votive for deliverance from the plague, Duke Emmanuel Philibert had it moved, in the presence of the greatest dignitaries of the day, to a special chapel in Turin Cathedral with a privileged private access from his sumptuous adjoining palace. The magnificent exposition was breathtaking in its pomp and ceremonial. This soon put the city on the map. It retains its fame to this day and all because of the greed of an obscure dean of an equally obscure church three centuries ago.

CHAPTER TEN

Savonarola Cries Afresh Against Rome - in the National Gallery

The continuous historical, that is Protestant, understanding of the Book of Revelation has powerfully indicted Rome throughout Church History. The Church of Rome particularly dislikes being portrayed as the Harlot of Revelation 17. She has frequently burnt such writings and, where she could, their authors.

The papacy is quite content for the Woman to be a picture of Rome, provided that it is made clear that either we are looking back to the Rome of Nero or that we are looking forward to a period of seven years great tribulation in the distant future at the end of the age.

Girolamo Savonarola

But in former times, if anyone dared to identify MYSTERY, BABYLON THE GREAT, THE MOTHER OF HARLOTS AND ABOMINATIONS OF THE EARTH with Rome Papal, retaliation was swift. One notable forerunner of the Reformation was burnt by Rome for his protest based on identifying the Roman Church with this passage in Revelation. He was the Dominican monk Girolamo Savonarola of Florence (1452-1498). A selection from his writings *The Compendium Revelationum* and the *Dialogue concerning*

Prophetic Truth together with his public sermons make his position clear.

He wrote in the last three years of his life: "Fly from Rome, for Babylon signifies confusion, and Rome hath confused all the Scriptures, confused all the vices together, confused everything. Fly, then from Rome and come to repentance ... Come here thou ribald church ... thou hast become a shameless harlot in thy lusts ... Thou art a monster of abomination ... And what doeth the Harlot? She sitteth on the throne of Solomon and soliciteth all the world ... He that hath gold is made welcome and may do as he will ... O prostitute Church ... thou hast multiplied thy fornications in Italy, in France, in Spain, and all other parts. Behold, I will put forth my hand, saith the Lord, I will smite thee thou infamous wretch."

"The Roman church is full of simony and vileness ... I visualised a black cross over Babylon-Rome with the inscription: "Wrath of the Lord" ... on the strength of this vision I declare again that the (Roman) Church must reform herself, and that very soon, because God is angry".

Martyrdom of Savonarola

Foxe, the Martyrologist, lists fourteen articles, all of a Protestant nature, for which Brothers Savonarola, Buonvicini and Maruffi were burnt in the Piazza della Signoria in Florence on the 23rd May 1498. Heading the list is, "Free justification through faith in Christ". Articles VII and VIII concern the prophetic identification of the Pope as Antichrist. The accusations were read out to the three men and they were given one more opportunity to recant. They would not. So, barefoot, with their hands bound, the three heard the terrible sentence read aloud by the Bishop of Vasona, deposing them from the priesthood and condemning them to death. "I separate thee from the Church militant and the Church triumphant". Savonarola, insistent on scriptural truth to the last, interjected: "Not from the Church triumphant - that is not thine to do". The men were strangled and burnt on a great scaffold with Savonarola in the middle of his companions.

Rome had silenced Savonarola. What is more, Rome appears still to have the power to silence Savonarola. The present author spent three weeks in Tuscany in the Spring of 1998, at the 500th Anniversary of Savonarola's martyrdom. Savonarola had not only declared Rome Papal to be the clear fulfilment of the prophecy of BABYLON THE GREAT THE MOTHER OF HARLOTS in Florence but also in Sienna, Fiesole, San Gimignano, Prato, Pistoia and Pisa. Sadly, although there was some activity in these places, it was extremely low key and far from obvious to the many casual tourists. Although some Savonarola material was available in English, this was not specifically to promote the Anniversary. The author came away with only one booklet in Italian produced specifically to commemorate the occasion. This celebrated his ministry in these places in art.

The Savonarola heritage

However, the Savonarola heritage will continue to be available to the general public, thanks to certain providential circumstances.

Firstly, although Savonarola's church, San Marco, in Florence, is under the control of Rome, the attached convent is the property of the Italian state and has been so since Rome's loss of temporal power. There is therefore unrestricted access, with generous opening times, to Savonarola's own cell, and also to his study, portraits, some contemporary Bibles and a large and moving depiction of his martyrdom.

The second circumstance is the prominent position Savonarola occupies (together with the three other great forerunners of the Reformation: Peter Waldo, John Wycliffe and John Huss) on the corners of the striking Luther monument in Worms. Rome has taken grave exception to this. She has objected that Savonarola offended against his calling, "by his fanaticism, obstinacy, and disobedience," so that the erection of his statue at the foot of Luther's monument at Worms "is entirely unwarranted" because he was not a true heretic. But she was unable to prevent Savonarola's inclusion in the memorial.

Sandro Botticelli

The third providence is in many ways the most fascinating of all. It concerns Savonarola's message and the subsequent effect of his martyrdom on Florence. This is the permanent presence in the National Gallery of the painting by Sandro Botticelli, *Mystic Nativity*, which is at the centre of a free exhibition *Kingdom Come* which will be open until 6th February 2000. It features both Botticelli and Savonarola. The importance of the exhibition to Protestants is that it shows that the academic world now accepts the link between Savonarola and Botticelli as an established fact rather than a mere theory.

In addition to printed material, there is a CD ROM *Exploring Sandro Botticelli's Mystic Nativity* which will serve as a permanent witness to the acceptance of this theory. The exhibition is rendered all the more timely by the fact that it runs concurrently with a much larger exhibition of Florentine art, *Renaissance Florence*. This chronicles, though indirectly, the rise to vast riches and power of the Medici Banking dynasty. From this arose Giovanni de Medici who, as Pope Leo X, confronted Luther at the Reformation.

What has made *Mystic Nativity* a suitable attraction for the millennium is the fact that is was painted exactly on the half Millennium in 1500 A.D. It portrays both Christ's First and Second Comings in cryptic form. This gives it an apocalyptic atmosphere appropriate to our present moment. But its significance for Protestantism goes far deeper than this. Even those who know little about art, are familiar with Botticelli's voluptuous images of the female form. Artists had little freedom in Florence. They were compelled to paint whatever their rich patrons, such as the Medici, asked. Alessandro di Mariano Filipepi (1444/5-1510) was nicknamed 'Sandro Botticelli' ("little bottle") from the family pawn broking business. He was a contemporary of Savonarola and head of one of the most successful workshops. He had made a great deal of money on commissions for the Medici and for painting the Sistine Chapel for Pope Alexander VI, who paid him "generously".

Botticelli's conversion

But suddenly, after Savonarola's martyrdom, his popularity declined. He lived very humbly and changed his style of painting to the sobriety of *Mystic Nativity*.

A variety of reasons have been advanced for this, varying from homosexuality to financial incompetence. But it seems that academics now agree that Sandro was converted by his brother Simone, who was certainly a 'piagnoni' or 'big weeper' - the name given to those who responded to Savonarola's call to follow his example after his moving martyrdom. The main sources of evidence are the diary of Botticelli's brother and *Lives of the Artists* by Giorgio Vasari (1511-74). Vasari wrote "Botticelli was a follower of Savonarola's and this was why he gave up painting and then fell into considerable distress as he had no other source of income. Nonetheless he remained an obstinate member of the sect, becoming one of the 'piagnoni' or snivellers (note Vasari's hostility - he was greatly patronised by the popes), as they were then called, abandoning his work." Botticelli had clearly heard the cry of God in Savonarola's condemnation of Rome and the materialism of the day and had come to repentance.

Mystic Nativity

The exhibition in the National Gallery contains a fine double sided picture, with a portrait of Savonarola on one face and his martyrdom in the fire on the reverse. There is also a famous medal from the British Museum which was coined at the height of his ministry in 1497. It bears a likeness of Savonarola on one side and the sword of God's judgement hovering over Florence on the other. The National Gallery exhi-

Savonarola Medal.

bition and accompanying CD ROM are the subject of strict copyright, as befits this age of digital reproduction. I have therefore turned to an earlier description of how Savonarola's apocalyptic message is hidden in *Mystic Nativity*, showing what a deep impression the message had made on Botticelli himself. Indeed, were the painting not clearly signed by Botticelli, there would probably be considerable controversy over the identity of the artist.

Colonel Young writes in his work on the Medici 1924: "That movement (the piagnoni) which exercised a permanent influence on so many others, had its effect on Botticelli ... (he) ... could only now paint pictures which repeated the impassioned Sermons of Florence's great preacher ... We have no more Greek goddesses ... The *Mystic Nativity* refers to Savonarola and to the state of things in Florence after his death. In an inscription written over it in Greek, Botticelli explains its meaning thus - This Picture I Alessandro painted at the end of the year 1500, in the troubles of Italy, in the half time after the time during the fulfilment of the Eleventh of St. John (like Savonarola he was a historicist and saw himself in the book) in the second woe of the Apocalypse, in the loosing of the devil for three (mystic) years and a half. Afterwards he shall be chained, according to the Twelfth of St. John, and we shall see him trodden down as in this picture".

Palazzo Signoria

The symbolism from the Apocalypse is rich and the reader should consult the National Gallery material. The usual scene of the magi before the manger merges into a last judgement theme. The three magi become Savonarola and his two fellow martyrs "slain for the word of their testimony", just as they were burned in the Palazzo Signoria. The devil's scuttling into crevices are seven in number after the heads of the beast upon which the harlot sits. Heaven is a golden sphere appearing as a mystical crown as twelve angels hold twelve prayers composed by Savonarola like the crown of twelve stars of Revelation chapter 12. Another painting in the exhibition, Botticelli's *Mystic Crucifixion*, from the same period, unfortunately only on loan from Harvard for this exhibition, "is an almost literal transcription of one of Savonarola's apocalyptic visions". Indeed, we can now say on the authority of the experts that Savonarola does indeed cry afresh against Rome in the National Gallery.

CHAPTER ELEVEN

The Origins of the Seventy Years of Papal Freedom

The official Vatican newspaper *L'Osservatore Romano* for the 17th February 1999 spoke buoyantly of the future of the Papacy in Europe. Under the banner headline "Europe Calls For A New Evangelisation", the Pope is reported as saying "The Old Europe ... now calls for a renewed Christian proclamation ... providing ... for the economic and political unification of the continent". To this end the Pontiff suggested that we "entrust our commitments and hopes to the Blessed Virgin addressing her with the title of 'Our Lady of Trust' as she is invoked ... in Rome".

Almost as if the editors were afraid lest some of the realities of the Papacy's role in the 'Old Europe' should disturb this optimism, the paper consigned its dutiful comment on the 70th anniversary of the signing of the Lateran Treaty to the bottom of the back page.

The Lateran Treaty

The Lateran treaty was made with the Italian State on the 11th February 1929, thereby settling what was known as the 'Roman Question'. *L'Osservatore's* article entitled, "Lateran Pacts Ensure the Pope's Freedom and Independence", claims that, "The Successors of

Peter have never thirsted for universal sovereignty". This is rather surprising in view of the haughty pronouncements of the popes of Old Europe claiming to, "hold plenitude of power over nations and kingdoms". *L'Osservatore* further reminds the Italian State that, "the presence of the See of Peter is a very high honour".

The old Papal States consisted of the central area of Italy and included Rome and the territory of Avignon and Vennaissin in France. Papal thirst for territory has been successfully curbed by Reformation influence and her possessions have never been extensive. The French territories were lost during the early part of the French Revolution in 1791. By 1861 all Italy, except Rome had declined the 'high honour' of having the papal territory in their midst. Finally, on 20th September 1870, Rome's gates were stormed and the papal troops surrendered. However, the then pope, Pius IX, proved intransigent and withdrew into St. Peters calling himself the 'Prisoner of the Vatican'.

Garibaldi and the Thousand

The history of the 'making of Italy' or *Risorgimento* ('rising again') as Italians call their unification movement, is a thrilling one and vividly chronicled by the great historian George Trevelyan in his *Garibaldi and the Thousand*. *L'Osservatore* pays lip service to the Risorgimento, quoting Paul VI's words uttered in 1959 on the centenary of Garibaldi's decisive Lombardy campaign, "Unity and freedom were the ideas that gave birth to the Risorgimento ... worthy of a people ... lacking nation and political greatness".

Nevertheless, despite a decade of feverish cleaning and refurbishing of Rome's basilicas, at vast expense, Rome's central Risorgimento museum, containing numerous inspiring exhibits, has been closed 'for many years'. It showed no signs of reopening when the author checked it in 1998. The Museo Storico Vaticano, covering the same period from Rome's standpoint, only opens two days a month, and that only for a few hours, in contrast to a recent large increase in the opening hours of the Vatican museums.

A whole generation of Italian school children have thereby been deprived of the equivalent of what to English children would be the opportunity to visit the Imperial War Museum. In contrast, Rome always does her utmost to keep her basilicas open to school parties. The author personally witnessed a large school party at San Francesco in Arezzo where a vast fresco depicting the lying wonder of the 'Legend of the True Cross' was totally obscured by restoration boarding. After being treated to a few sad photographs of the frescos, they were then handed over to the priest to be captive to his version of history for 40 minutes.

The Garibaldi monument on Rome's Janiculum Hill (not one of the seven hills of the Apocalypse) is off the tourist trail. It bears his famous words, "Rome or death", on the plinth and is a favourite spot for Romans trying to escape the oppressive heat of summer and the surfeit of papalism below. A canon is discharged every day at noon by Italian soldiers. This firing has become the symbol of a free Rome, although it was originally introduced by Pius IX to compensate for the chronic mistiming of Rome's clocks.

Pius XI and Benito Mussolini

Pius IX and the curia remained singularly uncooperative considering how decisively they had been defeated. The offer of a more than generous settlement in the Law of Guarantees, was rejected, thus delaying the solemn entry into Rome of King Victor Emmanuel until July 1872. *L'Osservatore*, while muttering about 'secondary ... objections', still gives as the primary reason for the delay as that, "It had not been agreed to - precisely - by the other party i.e. the Holy See", which sounds like a circular argument.

The stalemate continued as "Old Europe" passed away in World War I and the competing ideologies of Communism and Fascism arose. Achille Ratti became Pius XI and Benito Mussolini became Prime Minister, both in the same year, 1922. The devastating chemistry between these two, which was to work such havoc in Europe, is documented by Professor Kent of New Brunswick in his book *The Pope and The Duce*. Ratti's Jesuit adviser, scenting, at long last, the opportunity to avenge the "Prisoner of the Vatican", exploited Mussolini's ambition in a deadly partnership.

The signing of the Lateran Treaty.
From left to right: Rt. Rev. Giuseppe Pizzardo, Rt. Rev. Francesco Borgongini Duca, His Eminence Cardinal Pietro Gasparri, Hon. Francesco Pacelli, His Excellency Benito Mussolini, Hon. Dino Grandi.

No. 6 Piazza dell Pigna

The clandestine negotiations leading up to the Lateran Treaty were conducted by a go-between, the Jesuit Father Tacchi-Venturi, on the understanding that Vatican backing for Mussolini was dependant on his meeting Vatican expectations. The author has often stood outside No. 6 Piazza dell Pigna, reflecting on the machinations that took place there when the Jesuit Father first brought together Mussolini and the hard headed Cardinal Gasparri, having each threaded their way to this spot through Rome's narrow ill lit streets. The character of Gasparri as negotiator can be gauged by an incident involving the French Ambassador who accused him of lying. Gasparri replied that the Pope would absolve him if necessary. The British Ambassador to the Holy See in 1928 reported a serious attempt to assassinate Father Tacchi-Venturi in February of that year, confirming how much was at stake in the negotiations.

Creation of Vatican State

The 27 articles of the Lateran Treaty not only created the Vatican state around St. Peters (a map of the boundaries prefaces the articles), but it also gave extra-territorial status to St. John Lateran, the Lateran Palace, St. Mary Major, San Paolo fuori le Mura, the building for the Propagation of the Faith, the Holy Office (Inquisition) and the Pope's summer residence at Castel Gandolfo. Further, all other papal property was given tax exemption and immunity from state inter-ference. The Vatican also gained control of religious education and marriage ceremonies. A second document of 45 Articles hammered out the financial settlement.

Mussolini, in his turn, gained the assurance that "millions of human beings ... will ... look to Rome". He had forged an alliance with 'Catholic Action', the powerful political wing of the Roman Church in Italy, without whose backing he was lost. His upstart regime suddenly gained respectability even above that of Catholic Spain and the resurgent Catholic Austro-Hungary. There were other tangible gains to be had in the Middle East, Malta and Yugoslavia, the subtleties of which are found in Kent's book. *L'Osservatore* concludes "that the role of Catholicism is ... foundational" in Italy's national identity".

Il Passetto

An interesting postscript to this "enduring certainty" that the Vatican will henceforth always be welcome in the Italian State, comes from a disagreement between the Vatican and the Italian State over Il Passetto, the passageway linking the Vatican and the impregnable Castel St. Angelo. Mussolini would not allow the castle to become part of Vatican city. However, it was not until the 18th May 1992 that the Vatican was prepared to concede that the fortified passage between the two, down which many popes have fled to safety in times of trouble, was not part of Vatican City. Nevertheless, the Holy See still thought it prudent to demand a 19 year renewable lease on those 80 metres of passage that run through Vatican territory.

(Note: The Risorgimento Museum is now open and well worth a visit although it is reduced in size and part of the building is a modern art gallery.)

Il Passetto at the Castel St Angeli end.

Il Passetto. The passageway linking the Vatican and the Castel St Angeli.

CHAPTER TWELVE

Why Rome is promoting an obscure Marian Shrine

The headlines of *L'Osservatore Romano* (English language versions, 4ᵗʰ July) read "Mary, Bride of Divine Love". Either the English press were unaware of the importance of this statement or they believed that English readers would not be interested.

That was clearly not the view of Robert J. Dempsey, the editor of the English language edition of *L'Osservatore*, for in the following week he ran a further prominent article on page three on the same subject entitled, "Mary is image of heavenly Church".

These articles concern the Pope's rededication of what is really a comparatively minor Marian shrine in Lazio, just outside Rome, which has recently been rebuilt and modernised.

The announcement marks a further and important stage in Rome's progress towards becoming a cult of the worship of the mother goddess. It also illustrates an interesting trend, that of seeking to make Rome the centre of Catholic worship and the place where the supreme experience in worship is to be found. The Vatican seems to be promoting the Eternal City as the ultimate, complete pilgrim destination, like Mecca, and that in spite of the practical difficulties that arise from its lying within the Italian state.

Divino Amore

This *Sanctuario del Divino Amore*, or 'Shrine of Divine Love', is to be found to the south-east of Rome. It has its own listing, *Castel di Leva* (*Divino Amore*), in the timetable for the popular 218 bus route which runs from the Lateran Church out into the countryside. One suspects that millions of pilgrims enter and leave Rome without knowing of the shrine's existence and that, at least until now, this bus stop has been of importance only to local Romans.

In years gone by the shrine was seldom mentioned in the mainstream guides. A more specialised guidebook to Roman Catholic Rome, published in 1967 and written by a knowledgeable priest who was at one time a guide for English speaking pilgrims, is dismissive. He says: "I should not like to bring anyone out to *Divino Amore* in the expectation that he is going to see anything really remarkable. It is just characteristic of a small shrine to our Lady of Divine Love, full of ex-votos from the grateful but with no vision as its origin and no wide reputation for the miraculous". He then adds sadly, "It would not be wise to count on getting a satisfactory full meal" at this obscure destination!

The sanctuary was erected in 1745 to house an icon of the Virgin painted by an unknown fourteenth century artist. The painting came from the nearby *Castel di Leva* (home of the famous Roman Orsini family and later, the Savelli). The castle was destroyed in the 15th century but apparently a single tower survived above the Gatehouse and on this was situated the painting.

In 1740 a passing Pilgrim was attacked by savage dogs who were threatening his life. He called out in his distress to the Virgin who was naturally credited with his subsequent deliverance. In those superstitious times such antique images of the Virgin were considered to have been painted miraculously by the hand of God without human intervention. So the least one could do was to build a shrine where others might seek similar protection in time of threat or trouble.

This little 18th century chapel was approached through a small courtyard with the painting dimly visible above the altar. Romans love to get out of the heat and dust of the City in the summer and this probably accounts, at least in part, for the fact that the shrine grew in popularity amongst ordinary people. The grateful recipients of miracles soon brought their ex-voto offerings to adorn it. But the same can be said of every small Marian shrine and, had it not been for Pius XII, this shrine would doubtless have remained obscure to this day.

Rebuilt and modernised

As John Paul II explained in his dedication homily on July 4th (translated from the Italian):

"Today, the dedication of this new shrine partially fulfils the vow which the Roman people, at the request of Pope Pius XII, made to Our Lady of Divine Love in 1944, when the allied troops were about to launch their final attack on Rome, then occupied by the Germans.

"Before the image of Our Lady of Divine Love, the Romans prayed on the 4th June that year for the safety of their city; promising Mary that they would change their moral conduct, build the new Shrine of Divine Love and open a charitable institution in Castel di Leva. That same day, a little more than an hour after the vow had been read, the German army withdrew from Rome without offering any resistance, while the allies entered Porta San Giovanni and Porta Maggiore and were welcomed with exaltation by the Romans".

Mosaics of Pius XII and the pilgrim assailed by dogs were added to the old shrine, and a fresco of Pius XII's prayer with its vow was added to the parish Church of Garbatella not far from 'St. Paul's outside the Walls'. The custom arose of making a pilgrimage to the Shrine of Divine Love in the summer months. Commencing at midnight, from the *Circo Masimo* underground station in Rome, it reached the shrine in time for early mass - all of which may be of interest to local people but hardly warrants world-wide coverage.

Santa Maria Maggiore

What is even more puzzling is why the famous image of the Virgin known as the *Salus Populi Romani*, 'The Saviour of the Roman people', does not feature in the story. This image is to be found in *Santa Maria Maggiore*, Catholicism's chief Roman Marian church, inside its Borghese chapel at the top left of the north aisle. Whether painted without human hand or, as others believe, by St. Luke, it was apparently being carried in procession in A.D. 590 to St. Peter's in Rome by Pope Gregory to seek intercession for the city threatened with destruction by the plague, when God answered that he would save the City. This answer to prayer was confirmed by an angel which appeared in the skies over the pagan mausoleum of Hadrian sheathing a bloody sword. The mausoleum was subsequently renamed the *Castel Sant Angelo* or 'Castle of the Angel'. Subsequently a four metre high marble replica of the angel was mounted upon it. (The original is now to be seen in a courtyard. The present one is an 18th century bronze replacement). The annals of Rome record the numerous occasions upon which this image was subsequently processed in times of danger and legend abounds with further stories of deliverance. Why Pius XII did not turn to this image when Rome was threatened in the last war or, if he did, why Rome is so anxious to promote an unknown shrine, requires an answer.

Mystery of Mary and the Trinity

John Paul II supplies us with part of the answer himself, in his address at the dedication of the renovated shrine. He states: *"The 20th International Marian Congress will take place at this Shrine of Divine Love from the 15th to the 24th September 2000 on the theme: 'The Mystery of the Trinity and Mary'. I am delighted that reflection on Mary's unique role in the mystery of Christ and the Church is being constantly developed in the light of the Second Vatican Ecumenical council. This deepened understanding has its roots in popular devotion to Mary, and, at the same time, helps to nourish, elevate and purify it ... I hope that the adoration of the Mother of God will help every believer to understand the real meaning of the Jubilee now close at hand and to be inwardly open to God's mercy"*.

Whether this conference title suggests that Mary might be taking a further upward step towards equality with the Godhead, to celebrate the Jubilee, one can only speculate, but certainly such an important Jubilee event could not have taken place in the small outdated shrine that previously existed. The Pope recalled his first visit to the old shrine in 1979. He was given a gold olive branch to take to the great Sanctuary of the Black Madonna at Jasna Gora (Czestochowa) in his

Polish homeland. He must have realised then, that if Rome was to remain the ultimate Pilgrim destination in an age of unparalleled growth of Mary worship, it was necessary for the eternal City to possess a large prestigious Marian shrine capable of hosting global Marian events. In practical terms this would mean looking outside Rome's City walls. Large as it is, S. Maria Maggiore lacks Marian atmosphere in its main body and I have often observed the absurd sight of worshippers crammed into the side chapel of the Virgin of Salvation with a huge overflow spreading back haphazardly across the main aisle. Further, in the Borghese chapel the frescoes are obscure in their relationship to the development of Roman Marian tradition and indeed incomprehensible to unaccompanied pilgrims.

As he sat in the Marian Congress in Jasna Gora in 1996, Pope John Paul II must have derived considerable satisfaction from knowing that his dream would be realised in the year 2000. The sweeping, multi-coloured stained glass presentation of the miraculous Virgin image at the renovated Shrine of Divine Love and the airy circular appearance of the space, are reminiscent of the world's most popular Marian shrine, that of Our Lady of Guadeloupe in Mexico. Rome now has a fitting place in which to develop a new Marian dogma to mark the Jubilee.

World pilgrimage centre

However, as he sat in the shrine on the 4th July, it was clear that something else was also occupying the Pope's mind. He stated, "Today I would like to turn my thoughts to the many Marian places where I have gone as a Pilgrim during the last 21 years of my Pontificate. What a joy it will be for me, if next year I can go to Nazareth". At the time of writing, and despite years of Vatican diplomacy, no invitation has been forthcoming either from the Israelis or from the Arab States to the Pope to go as a Pilgrim during the Jubilee to any of the religious sites in the Middle East.

However, even if he should manage such a trip as a pilgrim, the Vatican must realise that there is no hope of its gaining any political control over the sites of the Holy Land in the foreseeable future. What is more, most of the churches are under Eastern Orthodox or Armenian

The Shrine Divino Amore.

The exterior of the Shrine, landscaped under grass.

The interior of the Shrine. The icon is the black square in the triangle above the Altar.

administration which is unlikely to be relinquished, even if the Holy See does move into closer ecumenical relations with the Eastern churches.

Faced with this reality, it has been very noticeable that the Vatican has been seeking over the last decade to make the Eternal City a more self-contained pilgrimage centre, rather as it was in medieval times. The development of the Shrine of Divine Love is presumably part of this strategy. Following the disappointment of not finding the bones of St. Peter among the excavations in the Vatican, an alternative crucifixion site for St. Peter has been restored, the *Bramante Tempietto of S. Pietro* in Montorio. So also has *S. Pietro in Vincoli* where St. Peter's chains are exposed.

New excavation of St. Pauls without the Walls has also been mooted. These could well uncover traces of the Apostle Paul to complement his supposed ancient funerary inscription *Paolo Apostolo Mari* under the high altar and his exposed chains in the Reliquary chapel.

Moreover, St. John is usually thought to have died in old age in Ephesus, but in recent years Rome has been renewing interest in the legend that he was boiled in oil close to her Latin gate, where the chapel of *San Giovanni in Oleo* stands to mark the spot.

The claim that the bones of St. Luke reside at Padua has been vigorously circulated recently. In appropriate circumstance, these could easily be transferred to the Eternal City.

It is noteworthy that the logo on the new *Catechism of the Catholic Church* is taken from the catacombs of Domitilla in Rome and some of the other illustrations are of Rome's key early Christian sites. The moves described above would help to reinstate Catholicism's centre of gravity firmly back in Rome, on the Vatican's doorstep, and within the fold of the European Union.

Our Lady of Revelation

Meanwhile we can watch with interest how Romans react to the fabulous upgrade of their Marian Shrine. They are notoriously independent characters and may well resent greater hierarchical control of a popular superstitious activity. As the pope himself said, these phenomena have their "roots in popular devotion to Mary".

Successful shrines are, by and large, based upon visions of the Virgin, and there is an alternative shrine of this type just south of Rome. It is near 'St. Paul's outside the Walls', by Trefontane Abbey, where St. Paul's head is said to have bounced three times following his execution, causing three springs to arise miraculously to mark the spot. The shrine is a cave in the hillside at a place where Mary is alleged to have appeared on the 12th July 1947 to a vociferous anti-Catholic tramcar worker Bruno Cornacchiola, and his three children. Mary told them she was to be called "Our Lady of Revelation". This shrine is crammed with ex-votives of working people, grateful for contemporary miracles. It has an appealing simplicity for working Romans. They could well resent Vatican attempts to "nourish, purify and elevate" their superstition and vote with their feet against the renovated Shrine of Divine Love in favour of the Shrine of Our Lady of Revelation.

Anyway, it could be easier to get a full meal nearby at Trefontane!

(Note: As everybody knows the Pope did visit the Holy Land. The diplomacy behind these visits may be covered by the author in a future article.)

CHAPTER THIRTEEN

Luther, the Papacy and the New Millennium

When first I was asked to write for the *English Churchman*, a formula was agreed with the editor whereby I should combine my interest in Protestant church history with the information gathered on my travels to the relevant sites, in order to throw light on current events in the Church of Rome.

In considering the grave news from Augsburg, where an attempt has been made to excise the heart from the Reformation, I intend to depart from my usual practice and work back from current events to their historical origins.

Undeserved significance

The start of a millennium seems to have clothed the signing of the *Joint Declaration on the Doctrine of Justification*, by the Roman Catholic Church and the Lutheran World Federation, at Augsburg, on Sunday 31st October 1999, with an undeserved significance. This day is known as Reformation Sunday. It commemorates the inauguration of the Glorious Reformation by the Augustinian monk Martin Luther who nailed 95 theses to the door of the Castle Church in Wittenberg, just south of Berlin, on 31st October 1517. These theses concerned the corruption of the Universal Church through the domination of the Roman Papacy.

The signing ceremony needed to fall on a Sunday in order to allow for a full weekend of official functions before its culmination in an ecumenical Sunday service during which the signing could occur. The 31st October 1999 provided a perfect prelude to the opening of the Romish 2000 Year Jubilee.

A Lutheran World Federation press release, dated 16th June 1998, indicated that the members of the Federation were to be given no further time to deliberate. Only 89 of the 124 member churches had responded, and only 80 had definitely assented to the document. The Lutheran World Federation was clearly embarrassed. It stated that, "though the Council approved the resolution on the *Joint Declaration* unanimously and without abstentions, it included concern for those churches who had said no or who have not yet responded". Gottfried Brakemeier of Brazil, President of the Lutheran World Federation, admitted to, "a certain disappointment that we are not able to finish the work as scheduled". The pressure from Rome on the one side and the ecumenical ambition of the World Council of Churches (whose Lutheran General Secretary, Dr. Konrad Raiser was a prominent participant in the signing celebrations) on the other, ensured adherence to the Vatican's agenda.

Papal delegation arrives late

The celebrations commenced on Friday 29th October. A corporate identity was provided by a logo on banners and stationery with Jesus' words, "That they may all be one" in brown emerging as a translation from behind, "Damit sie alle eins sind" in an ecofriendly green. The opening event was a carefully staged press conference with three channel translation into English, German and French. The most important Lutherans were on stage with Cardinal Edward Cassidy of the Pontifical Council for Promoting Christian Unity and his Secretary, Bishop Walter Casper, to make statements and answer questions. In the event the papists arrived late, disrupting the proceedings and missing the important statement by Lutheran World Federation General Secretary, Dr. Ishmael Noko, but ensuring full press attention for the words of Rome.

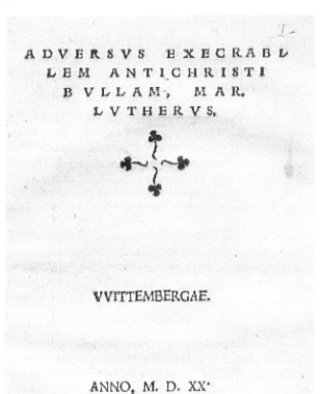

ADVERSVS EXECRABV
LEM ANTICHRISTI
BVLLAM, MAR.
LVTHERVS,

VVITTEMBERGAE.

ANNO, M. D. XX·

Luther's rejection of Leo X's Bull of Excommunication

Noko dismissed the Glorious Reformation in a few paragraphs. "By closing this chapter of Church History ...", he said, "the condemnations of the past" need no longer occupy us. The *Declaration on Justification*, "frees us to turn to ... the contemporary witness of the ecumenical movement ... It is a peace document ... The Year 2000 is the International Year of the Culture of Peace ... The divisions arising from the Reformation became the focal point for war and political and economic tensions throughout the subsequent centuries ... That division and those conflicts were multiplied throughout the whole world. The *Declaration on Justification* helps to draw a line under this painful history ...".

Source of Great joy to Pope

Cassidy was much more guarded and spoke of "very serious difficulties and questions," yet, "to overcome". The whole force of his subsequent remarks was to the effect that John Paul II had demanded some ecumenical progress on this front for the Jubilee and he was delivering a token gesture as a "source of great joy for the pope".

The highlight of Saturday 30th October was a ceremony held in the vast renaissance Town Hall of Augsburg. The Lord Mayor, Dr. Peter Menacher, addressed "hundreds of guests including Catholic and Lutheran church leaders, clergy and laity from various parts of the world, political office representatives, members of the armed forces and journalists". He called Augsburg an "ecumenical city" and the *Declaration on Justification* "a great stride forwards toward reconciliation". Dr. Raiser of the World Council of Churches told the same gathering that as a Lutheran theologian he was delighted to be witnessing the celebrations in his own language and felt it significant, "that confirmation of the *Declaration on Justification* takes place in Augsburg and before the eyes of a critical audience of German Professors of Theology, who have been critical of the *Declaration on Justification*".

Scarlet woman

The proceedings were crowned by a message from the German Federal President Johannes Rau congratulating the parties on their "important stride" giving "a strong push to the ecumenical move-ment".

The climax of the celebrations was the signing ceremony on 31st October at an ecumenical service held in St. Anne's church in Anne Strasse close to the Town Hall. The video of the event is especially impressive to those who identify papal Rome with the scarlet, bejew-elled harlot of Revelation, Chapter 17. The procession enters with ministers wearing sober reformed black cassocks and white collars, accompanied by reformation hymn singing, when suddenly, Rome appears amongst them in discordant scarlet, with Cassidy himself in dazzling crimson. He wears a huge gold crucifix dangling on the

Leo X at the height of his powers.

chunkiest of long gold chains in total contrast to the drab black clerical suit he wore at the press conference. The press described the proceedings as "colourful". The Rev. Christian Krause, President of the Lutheran World Federation, was completely overshadowed by this Prince of the Church. Cassidy's homily was from Paul's first Epistle to the Corinthians and was clearly intended to calm the fears of doubters. He spoke just like a Protestant, of building the Church on the foundation of Christ, without a word about Peter, the Keys or the Apostolic Succession.

Joyous uproar

The historic signing took place at 11.30 am and occupied four minutes seven seconds. Cassidy and Krause lead the dignitaries to a table by the pulpit to sign the Joint Declaration and sat together. The Lutheran music stopped and there was a moment of silence before a Latin chant struck up. The two men arose and left the table without a gesture. The two secretaries, Noko and Casper, signed next, and then heartily embraced to rapturous applause which lasted some minutes while the remaining Lutheran World Federation representatives also signed. Three of the signatories were ladies, "who expressed profound joy at being part of the history". Cassidy and Krause did then embrace at the call for the sign of peace and the whole congregation followed in joyous uproar.

Noko's first words at the Friday press briefing were: "It is appropriate that the City of Augsburg should witness this moment of reconciliation having witnessed the failure of efforts in 1530 to reconcile the disputing parties and prevent a split in the church". The following day, in the Town Hall, Krause said that, "A moment in history worth recalling is 1530, when Martin Luther's friend, Philip Melanchton, wrote the Augsburg Confession as a reply to the charges brought against the Reformation in the 404 theses of Luther's opponent Johannes Eck. But much as Melanchton was seeking peace and reconciliation, the Emperor saw to it that the document was rejected".

25 June 1530

The unaltered Augsburg Confession of the Reformed Faith, which was principally Melanchton's exposition of Martin Luther's doctrine, was presented to the Holy Roman Emperor, Charles V, by seven Lutheran princes and two imperial free cities, at the Diet of Augsburg on 25th June 1530. It is available in English in Schaff's *Creeds of Christendom*. The history of the Diet is to be found in D'Aubigne's Book 14, chs. 6-8. Twenty two articles present Lutheran doctrine in Part I. A further six articles in Part II outline the terrible abuses resulting from the domination of the church by the papacy, yet without naming it.

On August 3rd the Romanist theologians presented their *Confutation*. The Emperor subsequently refused to receive a Lutheran reply to the *Confutation* on 22nd September. Thus the Reformation divide was established and the true gospel cleared from medieval papal concretions for all generations to understand.

Melanchton, probably concerned about the possibility of war, had toned down Luther's words to avoid too blatant a confrontation with Emperor Charles V. Luther complained to Melanchton by letter, saying "I cannot understand what you mean, when you ask what we must concede to the papists ... we have already conceded too much ... I will not permit a single letter of what we have said to be torn from us ... I will not yield a hairs breadth". He later said, "Satan sees clearly that your *Apology* has passed lightly over the articles of purgatory, the worship of saints and, 'above all', of the pope and of antichrist". All the subsequent Reformed Confessions of Faith had an explicit article identifying the pope as antichrist, and Luther observed, that by omitting this, Melanchton had failed to erect a bulwark against Rome for subsequent generations.

Luther and Antichrist

The one piece of history that neither Krause nor Noko dared refer to during the signing ceremony was the fact that Luther had been constrained to take refuge from the fury of Rome in this very building. His audacious challenge to the papacy of the previous October 31st 1517 had enraged Pope Leo X. In those days it was a large Carmelite convent. Far from the prospect of a friendly hug from a Cardinal Cassidy, Luther was due to face a Cardinal Thomas de Vio, called Cajetan (after his birthplace) on suspicion of heresy. He had been ordered to appear at the Diet of Augsburg and had arrived "afoot and poor" on October 7th. He was still anxiously awaiting a previously promised   safe conduct from the Emperor, who was preoccupied with hunting in the vicinity. Since there was no Augustinian cloister in Augsburg, the Carmelites had kindly taken him in. Luther was also aware, from the burning of John Hus a century earlier, that Rome recognised no obligation to keep faith with heretics.

Pope Leo X had summoned Luther to Rome sometime before June 1518. A leading inquisitor - theologian Sylvester Prierias - had set out Rome's response to Luther's writings in *A Dialogue concerning the Power of the Pope*. In July, Cajetan had forwarded the summons and a copy of the *Dialogue* to Luther at Wittenberg. On August 5th, the Emperor Maximilian, in a letter composed by Cajetan, denounced Luther to Leo X as a heretic. Maximilian offered the power of the secular arm to enforce such sanctions as the church saw fit to impose. Frederick the Wise intervened to get Luther heard in Germany. On 23rd August, Leo X published the Bull *Postquam ad aures* directing

Cajetan to extract a recantation or send Luther under arrest to Rome. Luther stood firm under pressure. Therefore on 11th September Leo X published a Bull *Cum nuper* directing Cajetan to judge Luther but not to debate with him. Between 7th and 11th October (when the safe conduct finally arrived) Cajetan sought to browbeat Luther into recanting through the agency of his henchman Urban of Serralonga. Luther declared from his refuge in St. Anne's: "I hover between hope and fear".

Urban taunted Luther that he need utter only six letters to Cajetan at the Diet - *revoco* - 'I retract'. In the event Luther put up a magnificent defence before Cajetan. He defied Rome and returned safely to Wittenberg. Luther's writings show that after the Diet of Augsburg he became personally convinced that the pope is antichrist. He stood unwavering in this belief until his death in 1546. A preface to a commentary on II Thessalonians chapter 2, published that very year, plainly terms the pope "antichrist".

Luther's dying words published by Justus Jonas and others were, "pray for the Lord God and his Gospel that he may fare well because the Council of Trent and the insufferable pope are feuding bitterly with him". In his last will and testament he states how, "God entrusted ... the Gospel of his own dear Son to me ... a damned poor unworthy sinner ... making me loyal and true in that service ... (as) ... a teacher of the Truth ... in spite of papal interdict and the anger of the Emperor, of kings, princes and priests and of all the devils".

Now, 481 years later, those claiming to be his successors have betrayed that trust.

CHAPTER FOURTEEN

Antichrist is Walking Among Us

Some 20 years ago the present writer sent a letter to the evangelist Billy Graham concerning Dr. Graham's sad departure from Protestant principles and reminding him that all the Reformers, and those who followed in their footsteps, saw the Church of Rome as the great expected Antichrist.

The letter included an appeal to Dr. Graham to read what the Victorian prophetic writer Grattan Guinness had written concerning the Church of Rome. Included with the letter were quotations from Guinness' book *Romanism and the Reformation*. The words need repeating today. After all, Grattan Guinness addressed himself to only 200 million Roman Catholics, while we face a billion.

Grattan Guinness said: "Never was there a time in the Church's history, when she more needed the barriers, which prophecy has erected for her protection ... Futurism has crept into the Protestant Church, and broken down these sacred walls". "Futurists", he said, "remove these barriers ... Romanists, Ritualists, and Protestant Futurists are all agreed as to the non-applicability of the Scripture Prophecies to the Church of Rome and the Papacy". By 'Scripture prophecies' he meant, particularly, Daniel chapters 2 and 7; II Thessalonians 2 and the Book of Revelation.

Guinness continued: "Cardinal Manning says, 'The (Roman) Catholic Church is either the masterpiece of Satan or the kingdom of the Son of God'." Cardinal Newman says, 'A sacerdotal order is historically the essence of the Church of Rome; if not divinely appointed it is doctrinally the essence of antichrist'. Rome herself admits, openly admits, that if she is not the very kingdom of Christ she is that of antichrist. Rome declares she is 'one or the other'. She propounds and urges this solemn alternative. You shrink from it, do you? I accept it. Conscience constrains me. History compels me ... with holy confessors, with noble reformers, with innumerable martyrs, with the saints of ages, I denounce it as the masterpiece of Satan as the body and soul and essence of antichrist".

Canons Regular of Bodmin

Rome knows these things and she takes them seriously, even if, in public, she derides the Protestant exposition of the Revelation passages. The reproach of Scripture is ever before her. There lies before the author a first edition of Grattan Guinness *Romanism and the Reformation*, dated 1887. The first edition is much harder to obtain than the many subsequent reprints. This particular copy once rested on shelf 10, of section B of the library of *the Canonicorum Regularium Lateren-enesium de Bodmin*, that is, 'Canons Regular of the Lateran Congregation of Bodmin', who were clearly anxious to acquaint themselves with the ideas of Grattan Guinness, long before they reached a wider audience. These Bodmin monks were the successors of some who established themselves in England about AD 1100. They were directly connected with the Holy Lateran Church in Rome, which is, "the Mother and Head of All The Churches of the City and The World". Through pragmatic manoeuvring (described by Rome as being "not as faithful ... as might have been desired") they survived Henry VIII's destruction of the monasteries and were in a position to spearhead the re-establishment of Romanism in the United Kingdom after the Catholic Emancipation Acts in the 19th century.

Someone has studied the text and poured scorn on the words of Grattan Guinness in neat scholarly handwriting reminiscent of that of the medieval monks. Where Guinness summarises the unexpected gains of Romanism in his day, and perceives that, "the day has come ... to fight the battle of the Reformation over again", the critic writes scathingly: "How weak this 16th century heresy must be; not to be able to be proof against storms of persecution; how unlike this (the Roman) Church built on the rock (of Peter) in this respect; it is only 300 years and it has now to own its weakness against the Church of Rome". Incidentally, the observation that Protestantism "is only 300 years" old dates the comment. Where Grattan Guinness boldly indicted the Roman Church as the Antichrist of Scripture, the critic, unable to detect any weakness in Grattan Guinness' argument and having no cogent argument of his own, simply writes "Blasphemy!!"

Cardinal Giacomo Biffi

The present writer was not, therefore, surprised when, before the new Millennium was even a couple of months old, Rome attempted to set the prophetic tone for the new era. The front page of the *Times* on 6th March 2000, carried the headline: "Vegetarian Antichrist is walking among us". Here Richard Owen, the perceptive Rome correspondent of the *Times*, reported on the latest attempt by a Roman Cardinal to deflect the finger of prophecy away from Rome as being the Whore of Babylon. Owen informs us that, "Cardinal Giacomo Biffi, 71, the Archbishop of Bologna, said the Antichrist was not the beast with seven heads described in the Book of Revelation". This is a bold statement coming as it does from Biffi, "The leading conservative contender to succeed the Pope". The Cardinal was throwing down the gauntlet to Protestantism.

Biffi opposes the present Vatican policy of apologising for and repenting of the crimes of the Roman Church, particularly the persecution of the Jews and the Inquisition. He has found a supporter in the Roman Catholic historian Paul Johnson who resents the present "charade of bogus apologies".

Rome cannot err

In a book entitled *Christus Hodie* published in 1995, Cardinal Biffi explains his thoughts as follows. The Roman Church is always holy and cannot repent. She has no sins because she is Christ's mystical body. Sins of individuals are "extra ecclesial" (outside the Church). Biffi presses this distinction between the Holy Church and her sinful members and claims, "It cannot be laid to her charge if some members fall weak or wounded". (Interestingly, Pius XII, the Pope of World War II, was a strong protagonist of this view). Biffi would therefore totally reject the suggestion that the Harlot of Revelation 17, drunken with the blood of the saints and with the blood of the martyrs of Jesus, is the Roman Church, and must now seek forgiveness for these crimes.

Biffi has traced the history of this view, that the Church of Rome cannot err, back to the time of St. Ambrose of Milan, who said: "Non in se sed in nobis Ecclesia vulnuratur" ('The Church is wounded not in itself but in us'). Biffi repeated his views on February 8th this year in the opulent Paul VI Audience Hall in the Vatican. This was "in the presence of the personnel of several Vatican offices". Again he quoted Ambrose. Biffi's meditation was subsequently praised by Cardinal Sodano, the Vatican Secretary of State, speaking on Vatican radio. This is all the more interesting because ultra-conservative Cardinal Biffi seems as a result to have upstaged Carlo Maria Martini, the liberal Cardinal Archbishop of Milan, who is one of Biffi's most 'papabile' (electable to the papacy) rivals. St. Ambrose is greatly revered in Milan and his complete skeleton, dressed as a prince of the Roman Church, is exposed for veneration on his Saints Day.

Biffi's opponents

However, Biffi has his opponents. Avery Dulles, of Forham University, described in a lecture in 1998 exactly how the Vatican has walked this tightrope, exploiting her false doctrine of salvation in the process. Dulles says: "Theologians of both groups can acknowledge that while sin is present in the Church, the Church is not related in the same way to holiness and sin. It (holiness) exists most perfectly in Mary and the saints, who live according to the inner law of its being and exemplify its true nature. They are most receptive to the Church's faith and sacraments, and to the guidance of the Holy Spirit ... Members of the Church who fall into sin and error are less intimately united with the Church. Serious sin, indeed, erects a barrier between the sinner and the Church and may even in some cases result in excommunication".

John Paul II seems to have sought at one and the same time both to apologise for sin and yet, simultaneously, "to concede what Cardinal Biffi asserts about the holiness of the Church," and, "has at least once spoken of the Church as holy and sinful, but the Pope's normal practice is to attribute sin more precisely to the members or children of the Church. In addressing the symposium at the Gregorian University on the roots of anti-Judaism in November 1997, he spoke of prejudices and erroneous views in the Christian world and explicitly declared that he was not ascribing them to the Church as such".

The Roman Church is thereby excused from the Reformer's identification with the Whore of Babylon, even if her members seem to have behaved at times as if they themselves were.

So who is Antichrist in Biffi's view? The present world obsession with "feel good" causes like vegetarianism, pacifism, environmentalism and animal rights, will, according to Biffi, lead to the emergence of a single individual, a world famous philanthropist, who will bring about the "death of God" and the obliteration of Christianity. This individual will head up a world movement for environmental protection, human rights and ecumenism in a worldwide pseudochurch, where "vague and fashionable spiritual values" will replace biblical principles.

Cardinal Bellarmine

This is, of course, just the old Jesuit idea of a future single individual Antichrist. It originates in their commentaries on the Book of Revelation, produced during the Counter Reformation. Their views were popularised by the Jesuit Cardinal Bellarmine, who used his prestige to disseminate ideas taken from the writings of more obscure Jesuits and publish them in his famous book *Controversies of the Christian Faith*. Now, Cardinal Biffi is attempting to turn our attention away from the Book of Revelation altogether. He is, incidentally, stoutly opposed to dialogue with the Anglican and Orthodox churches because Antichrist will usurp them to his own ends.

Top: Bellarmine: portrait above his altar in St. Ignatius, Rome.
Below: Reliquary of Bellarmine's remains under his altar.

According to Richard Owen, Biffi's remarks, "appeared to mark out part of the conservative agenda ahead of the next conclave to elect a new pope," in view of the, "physical decline of Pope John Paul II". Biffi had been speaking at a conference held in Bologna, concerning the Russian philosopher and mystic Vladimir Segeyevich Solovyov (alias, Soloviev) 1853-1900. Solovyov was of Russian Orthodox background, but he promoted a one world Christianity in which the Orthodox church would be firmly governed by the Papacy. Subsequent persecution by his Church and the Russian State drove him to prophetic speculation. His present day admirers see in his work a correct forecasting of 20th century wars. His further prediction that Antichrist would arise amidst the international chaos at the end of this period has been exploited by Biffi, who insists nevertheless that a one world Christian system must be controlled by the papacy, and not be open to any ecumenical bartering, and certainly not to apologising for past crimes.

Russia and Papal primacy

Solovyov's book *Russia and the Universal Church* published in 1889 and translated in 1948, is an amazing defence of the papal primacy and absolute denial of any Eastern Orthodox primacy or claims to "quasi papacy" through the apostle Andrew in Constantinople. Solovyov maintains that the toppling of the true Primacy, that of Peter, firm upon the Rock of Christ's calling, at the Reformation, has been disastrous for mankind. "The nations and states of modern times, freed since the Reformation from (Rome's) ecclesiastical surveillance have attempted to improve upon the work of the (Roman) Church. The results ... are ... a universal militarism transforming whole nations into hostile armies ... inspired by a national hatred such as the Middle Ages never knew; a deep and irreconcilable social conflict; a class struggle which threatens to whelm everything in fire and blood; and a continual lessening of moral power in individuals, witnessed to by the constant increase in mental collapse, suicide and crime - such is the sum total of the progress" which a Europe weakened by loss of universal Papal jurisdiction "has made in the last three or four centuries".

What solution then does Solovyov offer to mankind? His answer is a re-established Universal Papal Primacy, with real teeth, eventually to overthrow the Antichristian spirit released at the Reformation. "The Papacy is a positive principle," of which the Orthodox east has been deprived. "This (establishment of the papacy as the leading world power) will involve the recognition of a historical truth now admitted even by Protestants (!), namely that the present day Papacy is not an arbitrary usurpation but a legitimate development of principles which were in full force before the division of the Church (the Eastern schism)".

Solovyov carefully details the Papal claims of Leo I, particularly, "The primary function of the authority of the Church - that of assessing and defining Christian truth, - belongs for all time to the Chair of St. Peter".

Could Cardinal Biffi be suggesting that he himself should be chosen at the next Conclave to lead the Church of Rome? And to lead it in this highly reactionary direction, as an Antichrist-vanquishing Pope?

CHAPTER FIFTEEN

Jesuit Educators Celebrate 400th Anniversary of the 'Ratio Studiorum'

Stonyhurst College, a Jesuit School near Clitheroe in Lancashire, stands in extensive grounds overseen by a conspicuous statue of the Blessed Virgin. This site in the Lancashire Dales was chosen so that the school might not be conspicuous. Despite the admission of girls and Protestant children in recent years, this exclusive, Roman Catholic, private school, is still Jesuit run. The fees are about £12,000 per year.

The College was opened immediately after the Catholic Relief Act of 1778 and 1791. These allowed Roman Catholics to have schools, "providing they swore an oath declaring that no pope or foreign temporal prince had any temporal or civil authority in the land". Even the Catholic Emancipation Act of 1829, officially prohibited them from recruiting Jesuits from among the students.

Operation Whiting

The main school is fed by a preparatory school, St. Mary's, on the same site. Following a most delicate police operation, code named Whiting, in 1999, the headmaster of St. Mary's, Rory O'Brien, and a number of other teachers, including three elderly Jesuit priests, Fathers Dooley, Taunton and Earle, were charged with indecent assaults alleged to have occurred in the 1970s and 1980s. Detective Inspector Steve Martin said that, "The Headmaster of Stonyhurst college and the Provincial of the Society of Jesus are fully co-operating with this enquiry".

When "charismatic and inspirational" Headmaster O'Brien was sentenced to a three year jail sentence this year, the Judge commented, "You are a humbug and a hypocrite. For 25 years you have been living a lie". However, O'Brien only served two months of his sentence because the Court Appeal overturned the verdict and refused the Crown permission for a retrial of the 1970s charges. His lawyers were reported to be seeking compensation and the removal of his name from the Sex Offender's register.

Appeal funded

Fr. Chaning-Pearce was convicted of molesting four boys in his study or in a tree house at Stonyhurst College. Since the oldest boy may have consented, the BBC reported, "The Society of Jesus ... funded his appeal against his convictions", in respect of this boy. "Jesuit Fr. Michael Smith said, The Society has a responsibility to look after us". Children's charities were outraged. Michelle Elliot of Kidscape said, "We just can't understand why they funded it. Why couldn't he go for legal aid like other people? I think that it does not bode very well for children who have been abused by a priest. They will obviously be frightened of disclosing this and think, They are all in it together". Fr. Smith said that Pearce was still a member of their family.

Aspiring Jesuit, Paul Von Hoensbroech wrote of problems at Stonyhurst as long ago as 1873. "I saw at Stonyhurst a laxity in education ... which ... does not redound to the credit of Jesuit education ... The instruction was worse than bad ... there is an elementary philosophy course ... each philosopher has a room of his own ... I learnt next to nothing ... I was soon infected by the idleness which raged with devastating fury among my co-philosophers ... It was an open secret that not a few "philosophers" made use of the easily granted leave of absence to visit brothels in Liverpool, Manchester and London; some of them even kept their mistresses in little villages in the neighbourhood of the college". He left the Society after 14 years.

Unfortunately for the Society of Jesus, which still regards the Jesuit educational system as its flagship, this scandal arose in the very year in which they were celebrating their educational achievements. The celebrations centred on the 400th Anniversary of their famous manual of educational method, called the *Ratio Studiorum*, 1599, or *Plan and Method of Studies*. It has been described as "the Magna Carta of Jesuit education". The celebrations started in 1999, but have been extended into the Millennium.

Paul Johnson

Ignatius Loyola, the Basque founder of the Jesuits, used the power of Jesuit Education to penetrate the strongholds of Protestantism in the Counter Reformation. Romanist historian Paul Johnson, a Stonyhurst Old Boy, explains that, "Ignatius did not really know what he wanted to do. He knew he wanted to fight the Protestant attack on the (Roman) Church. He was a soldier and he wanted to fight it with a disciplined force and wanted to create such a force. He did not quite know, to begin with, what they should do. His first idea was that they should act as stretcher bearer at the Holy sites and other shrines and look after the sick".

Johnson continues, "Almost by accident, he got into the business of high powered education and that is essentially what the Society of Jesus was and is about. In the 16th and 17th century, for any (Roman) Catholic prince in Europe who was prepared to fight the Reformation and fight the Protestants, he, and the Jesuits that followed him would provide a religious service. They would set up a University ... a Primary School ... Secondary schools, any kind of school from the earliest age up to early manhood. All the Prince, Court or Government had to do was to provide the money. The Jesuits would provide the expertise and the teachers.

The rigid Jesuit Educational system was supported by a system of internal spying and informing on fellow pupils to enforce discipline and was globally successful. In 1904 Schwickerath, historian of Jesuit education, was sufficiently confident to attack the educational achievements of the Reformers as a reputation built on the "rubbish and garbage" of historical misrepresentation.

Confessors and the Black Pope

But Johnson adds the crucial observation that, "After people had left University, they would provide a life time service of the Confessional. The Jesuits supplied very skilled, able, highly trained people who where the Confessors of the great, whether they were kings, emperors, princes, archbishops, cardinal, - anyone who held great power in society could get a Jesuit Confessor and the Jesuit would guide him behind the scenes". This information, obtained through the confessional, was fed back through the Jesuit ranks until finally it reached the Provincial, the head of one of the Provinces into which the Jesuits still divide the world today. The Provincials were obliged to write detailed and frequent letters, at least once a year, of all that they had gleaned, to the Jesuit General in Rome. Sometimes they used code or invisible ink. This intelligence gave the Jesuit Superior General such unique power that he was referred to as the Black Pope.

Claudius Aquaviva

The rigidly applied *Ratio* was introduced by the 5th Superior General, Claudius Aquaviva. "The *Ratio* laid out the organisation of Jesuit   institutions to the smallest detail". It tied pupils to the authority of the Roman Church and the philosophy of Aristotle and Jesuit morality, while allowing some intellectual freedom. The *Ratio* was "applied with undeviating exactness". Although "the single Jesuit teacher might not be the superior of the average teacher in good Protestant schools ... by their unity of action the Jesuits triumphed over their rivals as easily as a regiment of soldiers scatters a mob".

Loyola's shrine in Northern Spain, which the present writer visited in 1994, had a display concerning the Jesuits today. The statistics for education and allied activity are as follows:

Education:

This sector concentrates the majority (approx.. 24,000) of the Jesuit order, working in the following:

24 Ecclesiastical Universities
31 Civil Universities
46 Upper Education Centres
444 Secondary and Professional Schools
478 "Fey Alegria" (Faith and Joy) centres in Latin America
550 Miscellaneous centres

Publishing:

Books: Among its 50 publishing houses, it turns out an average of 5000 (new) titles a year. Magazines and Newspapers: In all some 780. A third of the magazines belong to schools and associations.

Social Communications Media:

35 radio stations, the most important of which is Vatican Radio, Seven TV Channels including one in Taiwan.

The majority occupation of Jesuits is still education.

The British Province

In the "British Province", thanks to our Protestant past, Delegate Fr. Alan Harrison only oversees eleven Jesuit Schools with 5000 pupils, although the Jesuits have wider influence through Roman Catholic Primary Schools. However, in the USA, where public figures including President Clinton are ex-Jesuit pupils, Jesuit education thrives. To mark the anniversary of the *Ratio*, the Jesuit General himself, Fr. Peter-Hans Kolvenbach, flew in on the 6th October to lecture on *Faith and Justice in Jesuit Higher Education* at Santa Clara University, Silicon Valley, California, the site of an original Jesuit mission. The Convocation began with a colourful procession of Presidents and Delegates from all 28 Jesuit colleges and universities in the States. They processed in full academic regalia to the accompaniment of triumphant music. Those taking part came from the oldest institution, Georgetown University, founded in 1789, to one established only in 1954. They were followed by the USA Provincials, the climax being the Superior General and his party of educational advisors.

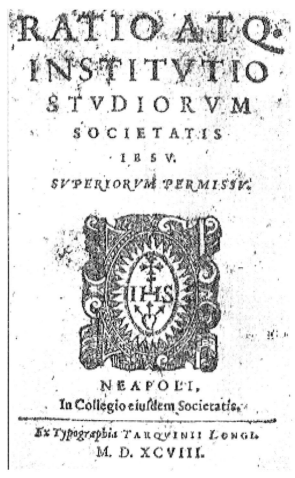

RATIO ATQ. INSTITVTIO STVDIORVM. SOCIETATIS IESV. SVPERIORVM PERMISSV.

NEAPOLI,
In Collegio eiuſdem Societatis.
Ex Typographia TARQVINII LONGI.
M. D. XCVIII.

Ratio 1698.

Fr. Schaefer, President of the US Jesuit Conference, introduced Fr. Kolvenbach. With humour - a common Jesuit technique - he made fun of "our enemies who think of us as this unified body, 24,000 strong, that goes out at the drop of a hat". He then referred to Kolvenbach's remarkable election on the first ballot at the time of suppression of the Society. He mentioned a Provincial who had apparently remarked that he was surprised at shy Kolvenbach's election, as Kolvenbach had said nothing at the previous General Congregation. Kolvenbach replied, "Yes - but I remember everything you said". Schaefer then revealed that, "This man listens to everything and he remembers everything. Ignatius in his entire life wrote 7000 letters. I checked with our Central Office. Annually Fr. Kolvenbach writes 15000 letters. He has an incredible source of information which is why the Holy Father, Congregations and Cardinals seek him out regularly. Other Superiors stop to visit him to ask what he has picked up, because, as hierarchical as we are, we are very grass roots and Fr. General's information comes from those letters which come annually from Jesuits throughout the world."

Ignatian spirituality

Kolvenbach's speech can be found on the internet at http://www.scu.edu/releases/1000/kolvenbach_speech.html. He attempts to embrace liberation theology and at the same time to justify the education of the great and good. He admits "Many raised doubts about our maintaining large educational institutions", to the detriment of, "direct social work amongst the poor". Kolvenbach clearly refuses to depart from traditional methods, insisting twice over a few minutes, "The real measure of our Universities lies in who our students become ... But the measure of Jesuit Universities is not what our students do but who they become ..."

Boston Jesuit College is observing the 400th anniversary of the *Ratio Studiorum* with a major Jesuitiana exhibition in the Burns Library, with a 1559 copy of the *Ratio* on display amongst a host of other rare volumes of the Jesuit's work in astronomy, physics, chemistry and theatre, which put the Jesuits amongst the powerful in those days. Since

Ratio 1932.

there is also an early copy of Loyola's **Spiritual Exercises** from which the *Constitutions* and *Ratio* proceeded, the Jesuits are seizing the opportunity to re-interest visitors in Ignatian spirituality.

A Counterfeit Gospel

The *Spiritual Exercises* are a Gospel counterfeit that Loyola wrote in a trance in Manresa in Catalonian Spain, and it was on these that he founded the order. They are instructions for a Spiritual retreat. Prof. Emeritus Jesuit Fr. Skehan who "guides the faculty and staff through" them, said, "This commemoration comes at a time of unprecedented ecumenical interest in the Ignatian approach to meditative retreat ... It is clear to me that since Vatican II an unprecedented and rapidly growing interest has been unfolding worldwide in directing and practising the *Spiritual Exercises* of St. Ignatius ... This resurgence has been stimulated in part by the recognition by Anglicans and by other Christians that the *Exercises* are an appealing and effective relationship with Christ and the Trinity". Apparently, some Protestant ministers have joined him as co-directors of retreats. Opus Dei may be in the ascendancy but the Jesuits are still a serious threat to the true Gospel.

CHAPTER SIXTEEN

Hang a Jesuit and He'll Make Off with the Rope!

"Film buff" Pope John Paul II is no doubt feeling excited about the re-launch of one of the old actor's favourite films, *2001 A Space Odyssey*. It was premiered in his own cinema on 1st March, thus affording him a front seat view of the big screen. Although it is a film that the Inquisitors deem "suitable for the faithful", it gives, nevertheless, a depressingly agnostic view of the future.

But in his euphoria, the Pope may have missed some news put out by a Romanian agency on the 4th March. Apparently, the left wing Greek film maker Konstantinos Costa-Gavras was due to arrive in Romania from Paris later that day and the news flash ran: 'Costa-Gavras "intends to shoot in Romania his future movie entitled *THE VICAR*".

However, rumours about this film have been around since mid-1999, when its production was first announced by a reliable Rome news agency. The equally reliable Richard Owen in *The Times* of 24th February 2001 ran a confirmation under the headline: "Film will portray wartime Pope as traitor to Holocaust Jews". So it appears that a mammoth attempt by the Vatican to suppress the film may have failed.

Rome v. Hochhuth

Anyone who is not familiar with Vatican power brokering would be amazed at the extent of Rome's influence in an industry renowned for its power and financial strength. According to Owen, the film is to be made despite "decades of disapproval by the Holy See". Indeed, Costa-Gavras could yet be stopped by the Vatican which has already frustrated earlier attempts to film the play. Owen reports that the original playwright, "Hochhuth, 70, a Lutheran who lives in Basle has claimed that previous attempts to film his play have foundered under Vatican pressure". Amazingly, Costa-Gavras is reported still to be hoping to "film in and around the Vatican". Could it be that, despite the financial windfall of the millennial celebrations, an impoverished Vatican treasury has overruled in this matter?

Santa Maria di Galeria

Under the headline *Vatican Electric Charges*, *Newsweek* for the 5th March 2001, revealed that the Vatican is not only refusing to recognise an Italian legal judgement insisting on the settlement of a $20 million water bill, but the Vatican is now declining to acknowledge electro-magnetic pollution of the air by the enormous Vatican radio intelligence facility. The residents of Santa Maria di Galeria, the adjoining Italian territory, are taking the Vatican to court with a hearing which has been adjourned until the autumn, alleging violation of the "stringent" Italian air pollution laws. Anyone who has looked across at this gigantic forest of aerials crammed into the Vatican and crowding the skyline, will realise that this is not a slight matter. *Newsweek* surmised that the Cardinals who have been summonsed, "probably won't even turn up". However, the Vatican may find its hoary extra-territorial status argument harder to sustain in a modern world. Some ready cash could then be useful. Perhaps Costa-Gavras had this in mind when he commented: "The moment was now right to film Hochhuth's version of the Pius XII drama".

Younger readers will know of the storm of protest that surrounded the publication of John Cornwell's book *Hitler's Pope* in 1999, which roundly condemned Pius XII for not speaking out against the

The Vatican building where Pius XII will be made a saint. The Palace of Congregation in Piazza Pius XII. The Congregation for Causes of the Saints is on the third flour. They decide on Pius XII's beatification.

deportation, gassing and cremating of six million European Jews. This book is in process of being translated into a number of languages. The author was reviled as a "lapsed (Roman) Catholic" renowned for his agnosticism when he was a seminarian. Romanists organised a boycott of Viking, the publishers. But what Rome really disliked was the publishing of key excerpts in well known international publications such as *Vanity Fair* and *The Times*. This provoked a front page response in the official Vatican newspaper, *L'Osservatore Romano* on 13ᵗʰ October 1999, entitled, "Setting the record straight about a recent book".

Cornwell's shock

Cornwell's claim that he worked "months on end" in the Secret Archive was refuted by a sinister documentary record of exactly how long he was there. The Vatican also denies that he had privileged access, pointing out that no-one has seen post 1922 documents.

Nevertheless, the fact is that Cornwell set out to exonerate Pius XII and it is clear that what he discovered was shocking, and enough to change his mind dramatically. The *L'Osservatore* rebuttal contained nothing substantial to relieve Pius XII of his stigma.

Hence Roman Catholics rushed to the rescue despite the fact that "no-one" has seen the post 1922 material. *Pius XII, An Agent of the Final Solution?*, and *Cornwell's Cheap Shot at Pius XII* by Jesuit Peter Gumpel, have now joined 20 other Romanist defences of Pius. Incidentally, the impartial Professor of European History at Columbia University, V.R. Berghahn, writes that, "*Hitler's Pope* is very difficult to refute".

Riots in theatres

Hochhuth's original play in 1963 made no pretence of being anything other than drama. The play, "the most controversial of the 20th century", was staged in an era of censorship and awe of the Popes. It caused an uproar throughout Europe and the USA in a way that is hard to imagine today. Black and white footage of riotous scenes in theatres is still about. On 25th September, 2,500 Swiss besieged the theatre in Basle and only powerful police intervention allowed the performance to take place. On December 30th, gendarmes had to mount the stage in Paris when Roman Catholics began attacking the actors. There were 30 arrests and substantial injuries. Vatican pressure kept the play out of Rome. Similar controversy occurred in the USA when the play opened on February 15th 1964. The disturbances gained banner headlines in the newspapers of Europe and the USA.

But even more striking is the film version, in black and white, with the sanctimonious pro-German Pope seated in brilliant white robes on a throne worrying about his investments and the state of the German and Italian economy. Pius is attended by Count Fontana, legal advisor to the Holy See and a Cardinal. Pius asks the Count how they are to attract major investment into imperilled Italian industry. Fontana replies that Rome's best investments are good, especially the holdings of the Society of Jesus. They gloat over cheques received from the Jesuits. But there is a dilemma. The dialogue reveals that the American Society of Jesus has grown rich by investment in armaments, producing bombers which might imperil Roman Catholic workers in the Jesuit mercury mines in Tuscany which in turn supply German armaments factories. Fontana wants the Jesuits to unload their Tuscan holdings. "At a loss?" Pius enquires. "Anyway, the Spanish SJ is selling mercury to Russia, and America is supplied by the Texan Jesuits, both at high returns, and they would lose their monopoly".

Prussic acid

This discussion takes place with Pius XII already aware of the deportation of millions of Jews to death camps where vast quantities of the poison-gas chemical, prussic acid, Zyklon B, are being consumed. Indeed, the play opens with Obersturmfuhrer Kurt Gernstein, responsible for supplying certain Polish camps with Zyklon B, risking his life to report to the German nuncio in Berlin in August 1942. Gernstein reaches the Nuncio's residence. A priest tells him to leave once and for all ... now. Gernstein replies that he has an urgent message for the Vatican, "that cannot wait a day ... not an hour". At Treblinka, in Poland, "Every day, Excellency, every day, ten thousand Jews ... more than ten thousand Jews, are being murdered, gassed". The Nuncio replies, "[Blasphemy] ... Be quiet! Go and tell that to Herr Hitler ... I have no authority to proceed ... against anything that is happening in Poland".

Gernstein's revelation to the Nuncio is dramatic metaphor for the voluminous information which poured into the Vatican through these same wireless masts that are now troubling the people of Santa Maria di Galeria. When R.C. Archbishop Emanuele Clarizio, member of the Vatican Secretariat of State throughout World War II, was interviewed a few years ago about "the Jews in the context of the links from the Vatican with the Nuncios", he said, "News filtered through every-where because wherever there is an (R.C.) parish priest, there is a collaborator with the Vatican ... that's what set the nuncios apart ...". When the play becomes notorious, Saul Friedlander, the Hebrew historian, surprised everybody with a book 'Counterfeit Nazi' in 1967, which detailed the life of a real SS Officer who acted much as Hochhuth's character did. But the drama would be just as valid if he had never existed, as history now identifies many brave Gernstein Characters who conveyed messages to the nuncios.

Attacks on Hochhuth

An internet search "Pius XII/Hochhuth" produced over 400 articles, almost all fierce R.C. polemics branding Hochhuth as the culprit to blame for all subsequent anti-Pius propaganda. We cannot tarry here to show that Hochhuth simply gave mass expression to what historians had already been demonstrating. Typical comments are: "the virulent attacks on Pius began with Rolf Hochhuth's 1963 propaganda play ... The recent slander against the Church and Pope Pius XII can be traced back to 1963 with Rolf Hochhuth's play, *The Deputy* ... These charges against Pius XII have been familiar ever since Rolf Hochhuth's play *The Deputy*, of 1963, which linked the words 'Pope Pius XII' and 'silence' ... Pius XII was a hero, but according to our own times he is a villain. That turn around can be attributed to the works of Rolf Hochhuth ... The attack on Pius XII took on major proportions, however, only in 1963, with Rolf Hochhuth's surprisingly successful play, *The Deputy* ... Only in 1963, when Rolf Hochhuth portrayed Pius XII as a Nazi collaborator, was the Pope accused of 'silence' ... We are still living under the impact of Rolf Hochhuth's very distorted presentation of Pius".

The bitterness of these attacks is because Rome knows full well the power of drama.

Jesuit drama

The Jesuits used drama for propaganda purposes throughout the Counter-Reformation. Their elaborate productions, mostly on the Continent, rivalled the contemporary public stage. By the mid-17th century there were 300 Jesuit colleges in Europe producing quality drama for propaganda purposes. Here the Tudor, Jesuit traitor, Edmund Campion wrote a drama for the English recusants, from hiding. Today, epics such as *The Mission*, *Romero* and *Black Robe*, made with Jesuits help, romanticise a Society feared by Protestants. The Robert Bolt play and subsequent film, *A Man for All Seasons*,

1966, engineered the most amazing rehabilitation of the reputation of Thomas Moore. The Omen trilogy of films, repeated ad nauseam on television, featuring the sinister future individual *The Antichrist*, with his 666 mark, has popularised a theological guess. Raw dispensational theology is complex, yet drama has made it a household reality.

Jesuit entering the Jesuits world HQ where documents were assembled for the canonisation of Pius XII.

The Representative, although exposing Pius XII, was also very critical of the Jesuits for their wealth and unethical investments. The Vatican, therefore, did not doubt that destruction of Hochhuth and his play would be pursued with all vigour when a formidable mafia of Jesuit Fathers, Graham, Blet, Martini and Schneider were recruited and "chained to the archives" for damage limitation in mid-1964. Unfortunately their first task had to be a hatchet job on one of their own, Fr. Fiorello Cavelli S.J. He had, to their embarrassment, written in *Civilta Cattolica*, the premier Jesuit journal, no less, as recently as June 1961, that in Spring 1942, "anguished appeals for help had reached the Vatican from the Jews and their governments in many countries, through the British minister to the Holy See, President

Roosevelt's personal representative to the Pope, the Apostolic delegates in Great Britain, the United States and Turkey and the Nunciatures in Romania, Hungary and Switzerland".

Jesuits and Jew

From then on, they vilified Hochhuth and became chief spokesmen in the media every time the matter of Pius XII arose. Behind the scenes, the Jesuits, who have spearheaded the Vatican retreat from anti-Semitism, are quietly distancing themselves even further from anything anti-Semitic. To that end the Jesuit General Kolvenbach opened the First International Conference of "Jesuits and Jews" on the 27th December 1998 in Krakow, Poland, near Auschwitz, by welcoming 39 key Jesuit educators in the field of Jewish reconciliation. On 30 December, a memorial service to commemorate the Holocaust victims was held on the site of the gas chambers of Birkenau, led by Rabbi Leon Klenicki, 'Peritu' (an expert) for the Congress.

In their final Report to the Fr. General, the participants raised questions for Jesuits concerning the encounter of Jews and Christians. Kolvenbach said:

"The fact that you hold your meeting in Krakow, not far from the shameful death camp of Oswiecim, should indelibly fix in your mind the stark reality of what hatred of Jews has accomplished and what we must seek in every way to prevent in the future. Most of us are educators. It is perhaps in this field that you can make your most important contribution to Jewish-Christian relations. I urge you to use the educational fora available to you to promote a living dialogue with contemporary Jewish thought, as well as to teach the serious sinfulness of anti-Semitism. At the same time, I encourage you to use the good relations with Jews that you have developed over the years to foster among Jews a study of the riches of Christian faith, not in an attempt at proselytism or to present Judaism as a failed or superseded religion, but so that Jews and Christians together can move beyond the conflicts of the past to a time of fraternal appreciation and esteem".

The Final report read, "We, a group of Jesuits who are educators, theologians, exegetes and pastors, engaged in dialogue with Jews,

Jewish religion, thought, culture and history in many different geographical and cultural contexts, have concluded a first meeting in Krakow, Poland. We have gone to Auschwitz and Kazimierz (the ancient Jewish quarter of Krakow). Together they symbolise the complexity of the Jewish experience in the Christian world; from the welcome by Casimir the Great in the 14th century of Jews fleeing persecution in Western Europe, to the genocidal extermination of the Jews carried out on Polish soil by the Nazis in the 20th century. Here we have been challenged to re-examine and affirm our commitment as Jesuits to the present reality and future of Jewish-Christian dialogue."

One recalls the Spanish proverb, "Hang a Jesuit and he'll make off with the rope"!